Evaluative Thinking for ADVANCED LEARNERS

Grades 3–5

Evaluative Thinking for Advanced Learners, Grades 3–5 will teach students to think critically about values, issues, and ideas while creating defensible arguments.

Evaluative thinking is a skill which helps students learn to weigh values and facts in making judgments. Working through the lessons and handouts in this book, students will examine difficult and ambiguous questions from a subjective and balanced perspective. This curriculum provides cohesive, focused, scaffolded lessons to teach each targeted area of competency, followed by authentic application activities for students to then apply their newly developed skill set.

This book can be used as a stand-alone gifted curriculum or as part of an integrated curriculum. Each lesson ties in both reading and metacognitive skills, making it easy for teachers to incorporate into a variety of contexts.

Emily Hollett and **Anna Cassalia** are award-winning gifted educators and instructional differentiation coaches with Williamson County Schools, Tennessee.

Discover the other books in the Integrated Lessons in Higher Order Thinking Skills series

Available from Routledge
(www.routledge.com)

Analytical Thinking for Advanced Learners, Grades 3–5
Emily Hollett and Anna Cassalia

Convergent Thinking for Advanced Learners, Grades 3–5
Emily Hollett and Anna Cassalia

Divergent Thinking for Advanced Learners, Grades 3–5
Emily Hollett and Anna Cassalia

Visual-Spatial Thinking for Advanced Learners, Grades 3–5
Emily Hollett and Anna Cassalia

Evaluative Thinking
for ADVANCED LEARNERS
Grades 3–5

Emily Hollett
and
Anna Cassalia

Routledge
Taylor & Francis Group
NEW YORK AND LONDON

Cover image: © Educlips

First published 2023
by Routledge
605 Third Avenue, New York, NY 10158

and by Routledge
4 Park Square, Milton Park, Abingdon, Oxon, OX14 4RN

Routledge is an imprint of the Taylor & Francis Group, an informa business

© 2023 Emily Hollett and Anna Cassalia

The right of Emily Hollett and Anna Cassalia to be identified as authors of this work has been asserted in accordance with sections 77 and 78 of the Copyright, Designs and Patents Act 1988.

All rights reserved. The purchase of this copyright material confers the right on the purchasing institution to download pages which bear the Support Material icon. No other parts of this book may be reprinted or reproduced or utilised in any form or by any electronic, mechanical, or other means, now known or hereafter invented, including photocopying and recording, or in any information storage or retrieval system, without permission in writing from the publishers.

Trademark notice: Product or corporate names may be trademarks or registered trademarks, and are used only for identification and explanation without intent to infringe.

ISBN: 978-1-032-21423-8 (hbk)
ISBN: 978-1-032-19927-6 (pbk)
ISBN: 978-1-003-26835-2 (ebk)

DOI: 10.4324/9781003268352

Typeset in Warnock Pro
by Deanta Global Publishing Services, Chennai, India

Access the Support Material: www.routledge.com/9781032199276

We would like to dedicate this book to all the students we have taught and will teach. You are the reason why we love this profession and wrote this series. We would also like to dedicate this series to our families, who have supported us unconditionally.

Contents

Acknowledgments		ix
Preface		x
	Introduction to Evaluative Thinking	1
	Materials	1
	Introduction: Frame of the Discipline	1
	Primary Source: Artwork Analysis	4
	Thinking Skills Avatar	6
	Bibliography	9
Chapter 1	Sub-Skill 1: Considering Perspectives	11
	Considering Perspectives Lesson 1: Understanding Viewpoints	12
	Considering Perspectives Lesson 2: How Personal Viewpoints Affect Others	25
	Considering Perspectives Authentic Application Activity: Merging Viewpoints	30
	Considering Perspectives Concluding Activities	32
	Bibliography	33

Contents

Chapter 2	Sub-Skill 2: Developing Criteria	35
	Developing Criteria Lesson 1: Personal Considerations	36
	Developing Criteria Lesson 2: External Considerations	41
	Developing Criteria Authentic Application Activity: Formulating Your Own Criteria	45
	Developing Criteria Concluding Activities	47
	Bibliography	50
Chapter 3	Sub-Skill 3: Assigning Value	51
	Assigning Value Lesson 1: Identifying Importance	52
	Assigning Value Lesson 2: Orders of Importance	57
	Assigning Value Authentic Application Activity: Writing the Rule Book	62
	Assigning Value Concluding Activities	65
	Bibliography	65
Chapter 4	Sub-Skill 4: Discussing Gray Area	67
	Discussing Gray Area Lesson 1: Opposing Values	68
	Discussing Gray Area Lesson 2: Exceptions to Rules	80
	Discussing Gray Area Authentic Application Activity: Socratic Seminar	118
	Discussing Gray Area Concluding Activities	123
	Bibliography	124
Chapter 5	Sub-Skill 5: Making and Defending Judgments	125
	Making and Defending Judgments Lesson 1: Evaluating the Choices of Others	126
	Making and Defending Judgments Lesson 2: Defending Our Own Choices	133
	Making and Defending Judgments Authentic Application Activity: Making and Defending a Choice	145
	Making and Defending Judgments Concluding Activities	155
	Bibliography	155

Appendix A: Assessments   157
Appendix B: Extensions   173

Acknowledgments

Special credit and acknowledgment must go to the many individuals whose work has paved the way for current educators like ourselves.

We draw great inspiration from the work of Sandra Kaplan, Alex Osborn, Sydney Parnes, Tamra Stambaugh, and Joyce VanTassel-Baska, whose curricular frameworks and research into best practice for teaching gifted learners are a driving force in shaping our own work.

Our guiding principles are grounded in National Association for Gifted Children (NAGC) programming standards, and we are so thankful for this organization's tireless dedication to gifted students, advocacy, and lifelong learning.

Clipart courtesy of Educlips. Used with permission under an extended license for hard copy books.

Handout font courtesy of Kimberly Geswein. Used with permission under a single font license.

Preface

The *Integrated Lessons in Higher Order Thinking Skills* series provides explicit instruction, targeted problems, and activities to teach gifted and high-ability students how to think using convergent, divergent, analytical, evaluative, and visual-spatial reasoning.

This unit was developed by and for teachers of gifted and advanced learners to provide explicit instruction in higher order thinking skills. In today's ever-changing, fast-paced world, our students require skill sets beyond rote memorization. Vast research supports the development of higher order thinking skills, including both creative and critical thinking skills which go beyond basic observation of facts and memorization. Systematically teaching these processes to students develops their ability to use these skills across the curriculum, building their ability to be "thinkers"—the ultimate goal of education.

The term "21st Century Thinking Skills" is widely used in education today, and while definitions vary, most educators agree: we need to be teaching our students not just *what* to think, but *how* to think. Learners in the 21st century must possess an array of thinking skills. They must be inquisitive about the world around them, and willing to ask questions and make mistakes. They must be logical and strategic thinkers. Logical thinking requires students to clarify problems while analyzing and making inferences based on the given information. Strategic, or deliberate, thinking requires students to think about where they are now in the learning process versus where they want to be in the future, and then determine action steps to achieve their goals.

Gifted and high-ability students require specialized instruction which is organized by key concepts and overarching themes. They need content which requires abstract thinking on a higher level than what is typically required by the general education curriculum. Beyond this, they require time to grapple with meaningful problems and derive defensible solutions. The *Integrated Lessons in Higher Order Thinking Skills* series provides scaffolded, focused lessons to teach these skills and give students authentic opportunities to develop these vital thinking processes.

Rationale

As Tony Wagner (Wagner and Compton, 2012) noted, our current educational system is obsolete and failing to educate our youth for the world of tomorrow. Wagner (Wagner and Compton, 2012) stated, "Students who only know how to perform well in today's educational system—get good grades and test scores and earn degrees—will no longer be those who are most likely to succeed. Thriving in the twenty-first century will require real competencies far more than academic credentials" (p. 20). Our educational system must help our youth discover their passions and purpose in life, and then develop the crucial skills necessary to think critically and creatively, communicate effectively, and problem-solve (Wagner and Compton, 2012).

Developing 21st-century thinkers requires a classroom environment that welcomes cognitive discourse and embraces the growth mindset approach. We must also teach our students that it is acceptable not to have an immediate answer; that some questions have many possible solutions, and indeed, some may never be answered; that persevering and being able to admit what you don't know is an important piece of learning.

Today's students must use metacognition, or awareness of and reflection on thinking processes. Metacognitive thinking is abstract in that one must analyze their thinking processes. Examples of this type of thinking might be asking oneself: "How did I get to that answer?" or "Where did my thinking go off track?" Learning to analyze the process of thinking is vital to problem-solving and learning. Teaching metacognitive strategies is a powerful way to improve students' self-efficacy, depth of thinking, and inquiry skills.

Students of the 21st century must develop problem-solving skills which require both creative and critical thinking. Creativity is a divergent thought process which involves generating new and unique possibilities. Critical thinking is a thought process which involves examining possibilities using a systematic, constructive method. Our students will be faced with unforeseen

Preface

challenges that they must be able to think about creatively, critically, and strategically to solve. We, as educators, cannot possibly teach students everything there is to know, as the amount of new information available in the world is multiplying rapidly. Therefore, we must teach students to be inquisitive, analytical, innovative, evaluative, and curious. Learning and applying these thinking skills will prepare our students to solve the problems of tomorrow.

While we know the importance of higher order thinking, it is often left behind the "testable subjects" such as reading, writing, and arithmetic. This series was created to merge higher order thinking skills and the academic content students must grapple with in school. Systematic instruction in higher order thinking skills coupled with rigorous academic content is a relevant and engaging method to teach the students of the 21st century.

Higher order thinking consists of several distinctive and sophisticated thought processes. Central to these processes are the areas of systematic decision making (deductive reasoning), evaluative thinking, divergent (creative) thinking, concept attainment, and rule usage (analytical). In addition, visual-spatial reasoning has emerged as one of the most important skills for developing overall academic expertise, especially in technical fields. Each of these central processes is addressed in its own book within the *Integrated Lessons in Higher Order Thinking Skills* series.

Focus Strand: Evaluative Thinking

Evaluative thinking is a critical 21st-century thinking skill and helps students learn to weigh values and facts in making judgments. This unit is unique in that it allows students to engage in productive struggle with ambiguous problems and scenarios where several answers could be considered "correct." Evaluative thinking is the ability to think critically about values, issues, and ideas to make defensible arguments. Evaluative thinking skills help students approach difficult problems with a critical eye and a balanced perspective. Working through the lessons in this book, students will learn strategies and specific academic vocabulary in five distinctive evaluative thinking sub-skills, applying each of these skills to new and complex problems. Students will engage in productive struggle with situational problems where many solutions could be considered "correct." The goal of this unit is to help students engage in this type of discourse in productive ways in order to arrive at solutions that they are able to effectively defend.

This book breaks down evaluative thinking into five distinctive sub-skills: considering perspectives, developing criteria, assigning value, discussing gray area, and making and defending judgments. Each of these skills is taught explicitly through three lessons, increasing in complexity and abstraction, and culminating in an application lesson and activity. This approach allows students to build their evaluative thinking skills incrementally and apply each skill as it develops. By completing all lessons in this book, students will be able to apply evaluative thinking skills and strategies to a variety of problems, situations, and contexts.

Conceptual Framework

This curriculum is targeted for third through fifth grade gifted and high-ability students. Each of the five Thinking Skills units will provide students ways to develop problem-solving skills which require both creative and critical thinking. Frameworks for questioning and methodology were drawn from several research-based sources, including the Depth and Complexity Framework (Kaplan and Gould), the Paul-Elder Critical Thinking Framework, Visual Thinking Strategies (Harvard University's Project Zero).

Working through the lessons in this book, students will make connections by thinking in ways that incorporate elements of the Depth and Complexity Framework, such as thinking like a disciplinarian, connecting to universal themes, reasoning using question stems derived from the icons/elements, and examining problems through the lens of the content imperatives. Students will develop critical thinking skills based upon the elements of the Paul-Elder Critical Thinking Framework by applying thinking standards such as logic, precision, relevance, and depth to elements of problems such as inferences and assumptions in order to develop the intellectual traits of a critical thinker. Visual thinking routines are also incorporated to help scaffold students' metacognitive processes. Each of these research-based frameworks is embedded within the lessons in the form of question stems, instructional processes, graphic organizers, and methodology.

Each unit in the series uses explicit instruction to directly and systematically teach students how to think. Research shows that the most empirically supported method for teaching critical thinking is explicit instruction. (Abrami, Bernard, Borokhovski, Wade, Surkes, Tamim, and Zhang, 2008). Using explicit instruction makes the learning outcomes clear.

Students are provided with clear, specific objectives. The unit lessons are broken down into manageable chunks of information. The teacher models the thinking skill with clear explanations and verbalizes their thinking process. Students are taught specific ways to reason and problem-solve. Students then practice the skills while the teacher provides feedback. At the conclusion of each lesson, students are asked to think metacognitively about their own learning.

Lesson Format and Guidelines

Each *Integrated Lessons in Higher Order Thinking Skills* unit follows the same format. Students are introduced to the higher order thinking skill through introductory lessons and materials to build schema in the targeted thinking area addressed in the unit. The introductory lesson in each unit provides a real-world connection. The overarching thinking skill is then broken down into five sub-skills. Each sub-skill is explicitly taught in three lessons. First, the students will be introduced to the sub-skill using an anchor chart. Then, students will participate in a warm-up activity teaching the sub-skill. Next, students will read and analyze trade books which highlight the sub-skill. Finally, students will participate in an activity learning to use the sub-skill. The third lesson in each sub-skill provides an opportunity for the students to apply the sub-skill in an authentic application activity. Key features of this unit as well as lesson summaries are outlined in Table P.1.

Unit Features

Materials

Included in this book are blackline masters of consumable materials to be used with students. Student handouts are provided with each lesson, and they include reading reflections, graphic organizers, full text stories for collaborative learning activities, formative "exit tickets," and others. Teacher materials, including anchor chart posters to provide visual cues for sub-skills, detailed lesson plans, and assessment rubrics, are also included. Other needed and optional materials are listed in lesson outlines. Links are provided for online resources, such as short video clips, and are accurate at the time of this book's printing.

Throughout the unit, trade books are used to teach and explore sub-skills in familiar contexts. These carefully selected trade books provide an exemplar for the lesson's focus. The recommended books are common and easily accessible; however, alternate texts are recommended to target each sub-skill (see Appendix B). Many of the texts may also have a digital version readily available as an online read aloud, accessible through a quick internet search.

In addition, some lessons utilize common classroom manipulatives such as attribute blocks, pattern blocks, or Tangrams. Printable versions of these manipulatives are also provided as handouts where they are used.

Preface

TABLE P.1
Unit Overview

Introduction and Rationale Teacher introduction providing rationale for the unit.	❏ Outline of Thinking Skills: Teacher reference explaining an overview of each thinking skill and outcome. ❏ Standards Alignment: Unit alignment to both CCSS and NAGC standards are outlined.
Thinking Skill Overview This section provides introductory lessons and materials to build schema for students in the specific targeted thinking skill addressed in the unit.	❏ Frame of the Discipline: Think Like a Leader ■ Students gain understanding of authentic uses for evaluative skills within a career context. ❏ Artwork Analysis: Students analyze two pieces of classic visual art through the lens of evaluative thinking to build thinking skill schema. ❏ Thinking Skills Avatar: Provides an ongoing touchstone for students to record key details and synthesize learning throughout the unit.
Sub-Skill 1: Considering Perspectives In this section, students will examine scenarios from various perspectives, considering how alternate perspectives might aid in building understanding.	❏ Lesson 1: Understanding Viewpoints ■ Students will work collaboratively to consider images from a variety of standpoints. ❏ Lesson 2: How Personal Viewpoints Affect Others ■ Students will consider a short video from multiple perspectives to determine how personal viewpoints may affect others. ❏ Authentic Application Activity: Merging Viewpoints ■ Students will consider a variety of viewpoints in crafting a new solution to a posed scenario.
Sub-Skill 2: Developing Criteria In this section, students will examine which aspects of a problem or scenario are important to consider when developing a solution.	❏ Lesson 1: Personal Considerations ■ In examining a variety of common situations, students will determine which considerations are essential versus non-essential. ❏ Lesson 2: External Considerations ■ Students will determine essential characteristics and considerations when grouping items. ❏ Authentic Application Activity: Formulating Your Own Criteria ■ Students will work to develop their own criteria in crafting a personal solution to an authentic problem.

(Continued)

TABLE P.1
(Continued)

Sub-Skill 3: Assigning Value In this section students develop strategies for determining weighted values when seeking solution paths.	❏ Lesson 1: Identifying Importance ■ Students consider various familiar objects and consider the most important/essential characteristics. ❏ Lesson 2: Orders of Importance ■ Students work in a cross-curricular context to rank items in groups based on orders of importance. ❏ Authentic Application Activity: Writing the Rule Book ■ Students work to develop a set of rules that are the most important in governing their classrooms.
Sub-Skill 4: Discussing Gray Area Students will work with ambiguous problems and scenarios to develop skills for reasoning through problems with no clear "correct" answer.	❏ Lesson 1: Opposing Values ■ Students reason through scenarios where two values are in conflict, citing text evidence and self-developed criteria to make claims. ❏ Lesson 2: Exceptions to Rules ■ Students work with classic literature to examine situations in which there might be exceptions to widely accepted rules, justifying their claims through text evidence. ❏ Authentic Application Activity: Socratic Seminar ■ Students collaboratively discuss gray area found in classic fairytales.
Sub-Skill 5: Making and Defending Judgments Students will work through a variety of activities and models to understand how reflection plays a part in problem-solving.	❏ Lesson 1: Evaluating the Choices of Others ■ Students examine choices of literary characters, determining probable criteria and lines of reasoning. ❏ Lesson 2: Defending Our Own Choices ■ Students learn the Evaluation Matrix strategy for analyzing and ranking solution options based on quantitative criteria. ❏ Authentic Application Activity: Making and Defending a Choice ■ Students apply all skills learned in this unit to a problem-based scenario that asks them to rank the "best" toy and then defend their stance.
Appendix A **Appendix B**	❏ Assessment Options ❏ Extension Options

Preface

Teacher's note: It is always recommended that teachers preview any content (books, videos, images, etc.) before implementing it with students. Be sure to consider the context of the classroom and/or school in which the materials are to be used, being sensitive to the needs, experiences, and diversity of the students. Where possible, alternate trade books are suggested. Links provided are known to be accurate at the time of this book's publication.

Assessments

Possible *answer keys* and suggested *key understandings* are provided throughout the unit. These sample answers were created to help the teacher see the intended purpose for each lesson and illustrate the thinking skills students should be mastering. However, due to the open-ended nature of many of the lessons and activities, these answers should only be used as a guide and variations should be encouraged.

Blackline masters of assessment options are provided in Appendix A. Formative assessments are provided throughout the unit in the form of an exit ticket to conclude each sub-skill section. An overall unit rubric is provided along with diagnostic guidelines for observation. A whole-group checklist is provided for each sub-skill with diagnostic guidelines included. Teachers should review and select assessment options that best meet their goals for their students. It is recommended that students be assessed using a mastery mindset; growth in thinking skills is an ongoing process and all progress should be celebrated and acknowledged.

Time Allotment

Each lesson in this unit is intended to be taught in 60–90 minutes, but some lessons may take less or more time. In general, this unit can be taught in 15–20 hours of instructional time.

Unit Goals and Objectives

Concept

To develop conceptual awareness of evaluative thinking skills using cross-curricular lessons, the students will:

- ❏ Develop an understanding of how personal perspectives shape our thinking

- Learn methods developing criteria when forming solution paths
- Understand that potential solutions may be more or less important depending on unique situations
- Develop tolerance for engaging in productive struggle when questions do not have clear solutions
- understand that solving problems requires determining a defensible solution

Process

To develop deductive reasoning based on critical observation, valid evidence, and inferencing skills to determine a single correct answer, the students will:

- Identify and examine unique perspectives and their implications
- Examine both internal and external considerations in order to develop criteria for solving problems
- Rank potential solutions in orders of importance, assigning value to various elements
- Engage in productive struggle and academic discourse with situations that are ambiguous
- Choose and carry out a chosen solution path
- Defend choices and judgments with solid rationale, both quantitative and qualitative
- Apply evidence to support explanations

Standards Alignment

Common Core State Standards (CCSS)

Standards are aligned with each of the five thinking skills targeted in the series *Integrated Lessons in Higher Order Thinking Skills*. Specific thinking skills are noted using the following key (see also Table P.2):

- A: Analytical Thinking
- C: Convergent Thinking
- D: Divergent Thinking
- E: Evaluative Thinking
- V: Visual-Spatial Thinking

TABLE P.2
CCSS Alignment

Language Standards	CCR Anchor Standards for Reading *1, 6, 7, 8*	❏ Draw logical inferences from text (C/E) ❏ Cite text evidence to support claims (C/E) ❏ Assess perspectives (A/C/D/E/V) ❏ Evaluate various content formats (A/C/D/E/V) ❏ Evaluate arguments based on evidence (E)
	CCR Anchor Standards for Writing *1, 3, 4, 8, 9, 10*	❏ Write arguments, citing text evidence and using valid reasoning (C/E) ❏ Write narratives (D) ❏ Develop written work appropriate to a variety of tasks (A/C/D/E/V) ❏ Evaluate and synthesize information from a variety of sources (E) ❏ Draw evidence to support analysis (A) ❏ Write routinely and for many purposes (A/C/D/E/V)
	CCR Anchor Standards for Speaking and Listening *1, 2, 3, 4*	❏ Collaborate for a variety of purposes with a variety of partners (A/C/D/E/V) ❏ Integrate information from a variety of sources (A/C/D/E/V) ❏ Critically evaluate speakers' perspectives (E) ❏ Present information, including evidence, in ways that allow others to follow lines of reasoning (A/C/E)
	CCR Anchor Standards for Language *3, 5, 6*	❏ Make effective use of appropriate language in a variety of contexts (A/C/D/E/V) ❏ Understand and make use of figurative language (A/D/E) ❏ Develop and apply academic vocabulary (A/C/D/E/V)
Mathematics Standards	CCSS for Mathematics: Practice Standards	❏ Make sense of problems and persevere in solving them ❏ Reason abstractly and quantitatively ❏ Construct viable arguments and critique the reasoning of others ❏ Model with mathematics ❏ Use appropriate tools strategically ❏ Attend to precision ❏ Look for and make use of structure ❏ Look for and express regularity in repeated reasoning *Applicable to problems presented in all Thinking Skills units.*

(Continued)

TABLE P.2
(Continued)

	CCSS for Mathematics: Operations and Algebraic Thinking 2.OA, 3.OA, 4.OA, 5.OA	❏ Generate and analyze patterns and relationships (A/C/V) ❏ Represent problems both concretely and abstractly (A/C/V)
	CCSS for Mathematics: Measurement and Data 2.MD, 3.MD, 4.MD, 5.MD	❏ Represent and interpret data (A/C/V)
	CCSS for Mathematics: Geometry 2.G, 3.G, 4.G, 5.G	❏ Solve problems involving the coordinate plane (V) ❏ Solve problems involving lines, angles, and dimensions (V) ❏ Reason with shapes and their attributes (V)

NAGC Programming Standards Alignment

Teaching thinking skills aligns with NAGC Gifted programming standards as best practice for gifted students:

- ❏ **Standard 1**: Students create awareness of and interest in their learning and cognitive growth
- ❏ **Standard 2**: Thinking skill aligned assessments provide evidence of learning progress
- ❏ **Standard 3**: Explicit instruction in thinking skills and metacognitive strategies is research-based best practice and meets the needs of gifted students for opportunities to develop depth, complexity, and abstraction in thinking and inquiry
- ❏ **Standard 5**: Competence in thinking skills promotes cognitive, social-emotional, and psychosocial development of students

Bibliography

Abrami, P.C., Bernard, R.M., Borokhovski, E., Wade, A., Surkes, M.A., Tamim, R., and Zhang, D. (2008). Instructional interventions affecting critical thinking skills and dispositions: A stage 1 meta-analysis. *Review of Educational Research*, 78(4), 1102–1134.

Common Core State Standards Initiative. (2022a). Common core state standards for mathematics. http://www.corestandards.org/wp-content/uploads/Math_Standards1.pdf.

Common Core State Standards Initiative. (2022b). Common core state standards for English language arts & literacy in history/social studies, science, and technical subjects. http://www.corestandards.org/wp-content/uploads/ELA_Standards1.pdf.

Dweck, C.S. (2006). *Mindset: The new psychology of success*. New York: Random House.

Kaplan, S. and Gould, B. (1995, 2003). *Depth & complexity icons, OERI, Javits project T.W.O. 2. Educator to educator. LVI*. J. Taylor Education, 2016.

NAGC Professional Standards Committee. (2018–2019). 2019 Pre-K-grade 12 gifted programming standards. https://www.nagc.org/sites/default/files/standards/Intro%202019%20Programming%20Standards.pdf.

Paul, R., and Elder, L. (2020). *The miniature guide to critical thinking concepts and tools*. Santa Barbara, CA: Foundation for Critical Thinking.

Tishman, S., MacGillivray, D., and Palmer, P. (1999). Investigating the educational impact & potential of the MoMA's visual thinking curriculum. http://www.pz.harvard.edu/projects/momas-visual-thinking-curriculum-project.

Wagner, T., and Compton, R.A. (2012). *Creating innovators: The making of young people who will change the world*. New York: Scribner.

Introduction to Evaluative Thinking

Key Question: What is evaluative thinking?

Materials

- Handout I.1: Evaluative Thinking: Do It Like a Leader! (one per student)
- Handout I.2: About the Artwork (one for display or one per student)
- Primary Source Artwork to Display:
  - *Still Life with Flowers* by Ambrosius Bosschaert (1617): https://artsandculture.google.com/asset/still-life-with-flowers-ambrosius-bosschaert-the-elder/UgGmKyl0WuuDEA?hl=en
  - *Irises* by Vincent van Gogh (1890): https://www.metmuseum.org/art/collection/search/436528
- Handout I.3: Artwork Analysis (one per student)
- Handout I.4: Evaluative Thinking Avatar (one per student)

Introduction: Frame of the Discipline

- Tell students they will be learning how to think using *evaluative* reasoning. *Evaluative thinking* means thinking through tricky problems using criteria and values to make and defend a solution.
- Read together the article Evaluative Thinking: Do It Like a Leader! (Handout I.1a).
- Model answering the questions on the sheet Framing the Thinking of a Leader (Handout I.1b). See key understandings to target in Box I.1.

DOI: 10.4324/9781003268352-1

Handout I.1a: Evaluative Thinking Like a Leader

Name: _____

Leaders come in many shapes and sizes and can be found in all areas of life. People look to leaders to help guide them in the right directions. Think about some leaders you know: your school's principal, your teacher, the owner of a company, the mayor of your town, or the president of the United States of America. These leaders each have very different jobs to do, but they all have one thinking skill they use each day in their job: **evaluative thinking.** Evaluative thinking is a special kind of thinking that helps us think through decisions and make good choices.

Leaders must make many decisions each day. They have to think through what will be the best plan of action for the people or system they are responsible for leading. To make sure they're making the best decision they can, they must first **CONSIDER PERSPECTIVES**, or think about who would have an opinion or be affected by an action/choice. Keeping in mind how our choices and opinions affect others helps leaders make fair choices.

Leaders must also look at each problem that arises carefully, **DEVELOPING CRITERIA** and **ASSIGNING VALUE** to possible solutions. Leaders must consider what the most important aspects of each problem might be, and then think of solutions with the lens of what is most important. This can change from problem to problem, but good leaders are able to analyze considerations and think through priorities.

If this sounds tricky, that's because it is! There is often not one single correct answer to a question. Leaders must **CONSIDER GRAY AREA**, or think about problems that don't have clear right/wrong solutions. When there is more than one solution that could work for a problem, leaders must consider which solution will be the *best*, even when more than one solution could work.

Leaders are also responsible for **MAKING DECISIONS** and **DEFENDING JUDGEMENTS**. Leaders must eventually make choices, even when those decisions are tough calls. Once the decision is made, leaders must be able to rely on the perspectives, criteria, and values they considered to defend, or support their decision.

It's not easy to be a leader but developing your evaluative thinking skills can help you work through some of the tougher choices a leader makes every day.

Handout I.1b: Framing the Thinking of a Leader

Name: _____

What questions do leaders ask?	What tools or thinking skills does a leader need?

Describe the main purpose of a leader.

Why are leaders important in today's world?	How do leader think about new information?

EVALUATIVE THINKING for Advanced Learners, Grades 3–5

> ### Box I.1: Framing the Thinking of a Leader Key Understandings
>
> - *What questions do leaders ask?*
>   - What are the considerations?
>   - What are the consequences?
>   - Who is this important to?
>   - What is most important?
> - *What tools or thinking skills does a leader need?*
>   - Knowledge of people whom they are leading and their perspectives.
>   - Able to organize information to defend their thinking.
>   - Able to evaluate what is fair, ethical, and beneficial.
> - *Why are leaders important in today's world?*
>   - Leaders guide groups. They make sure that decisions are made which reflect the perspectives, needs, and wants of those whom they serve. Without leaders, many tasks would not get accomplished.
> - *How do leaders think about new information?*
>   - Leaders consider various perspectives and gather as much information as possible.
>   - Leaders consider what is most important in the long, medium, and short term.
> - *Describe the main purpose of a leader.*
>   - Leaders guide people. They make decisions and help others take action to implement those decisions.

- Tell students that throughout this unit they will be thinking like a leader to solve problems using criteria and to defend their solutions.

Primary Source: Artwork Analysis

- Show students the About the Artwork page (Handout I.2). You may choose to either duplicate and distribute copies to each student or simply use a document camera to share one class copy. Shown are two images of flowers in vases along with some background information about the two paintings. Read the information about each painting

Handout I.2: About the Artwork

Name: _____

Ambrosius Bosschaert was a Dutch painter. He is most famous for his still life paintings of flowers. His three main motifs are flowers in a vase on a table, in a niche, or on a windowsill. His manner of painting included symmetrical, aligned bouquets with various flowers. His technique was more natural painting petals with soft texture and subtle tones in the background. He often painted on copper which enhanced the precise technique and gave a brilliance to the flowers.

His most expensive painting sold to date was auctioned for $4.6 million dollars.

Still Life with Flowers by Ambrosius Bosschaert (1617)

Vincent Van Gogh is one of the most famous post-impressionist artists. Van Gogh lived a troubled life with bouts of insanity. His technique used a passionate brush stroke, intense colors, surface tension, and movement in line and form. His powerful use of color and thickly laid on paint added a special texture to his paintings. During his lifetime he sold only one painting however, his legacy lives on having left a lasting impact on modern art. He is viewed as one of the most influential artists.

Irises by Vincent Van Gogh (1890)

His most expensive painting sold to date was a portrait of Dr. Gachet in 1990 at $82.5 million dollars.

- aloud with students. Invite students to turn and talk to a partner about what they found interesting or surprising in the article.
- ❏ Display each piece of artwork in a format that allows students to consider the detail, color, technique, and overall impression of each. Links to digitized versions of each piece of artwork are provided in the materials section, and it is recommended that the artwork be projected or enlarged to allow students to view it clearly.
- ❏ Guide students in sharing their opinions about the value of each piece of artwork. Probe for reasoning: "Why do you think what you do?"
- ❏ Discuss with students that we, as consumers of artwork, are always entitled to our own opinions. We do base these opinions on certain considerations, or criteria, such as what we like, our favorite colors, and our own bias.
- ❏ Give students the Primary Source: Artwork Analysis page (Handout I.3). Guide students through answering each section on the page. Key understandings from the artwork analysis are outlined in Table I.1. Note that opinions and ratings should be each student's own thinking; some considerations are included to help the teacher facilitate discussion.
- ❏ Remind students they are using evaluative thinking when comparing these paintings. They thought about what was important, valuable, interesting, and unique about each work in order to make a determination about which was "better." Even though the stance students take here is not what we might consider a true right/wrong solution, they are able to defend it based upon their thinking.

Thinking Skills Avatar

- ❏ The final introductory lesson involves students creating their own Evaluative Thinking Avatar. Today, students will decorate their Avatar. Distribute Handout I.4.
- ❏ Discuss with students the concept of an avatar. An avatar is a symbolic representation of a person that can be used as a stand-in. As you move through the evaluative thinking sub-skills in this unit, this page will serve as a touch point for students to connect the skills together into one representation of evaluative thinking.
- ❏ Explain that throughout this unit they will be introduced to five learning targets:
    - ■ Considering Perspectives
    - ■ Developing Criteria
    - ■ Assigning Value

Handout I.3: Artwork Analysis

Name: _____

| *Still Life with Flowers* by Ambrosius Bosschaert (1617) | *Irises* by Vincent Van Gogh (1890) |

FACTS
- What do we know about this painting?
- What type of painting is this?
- Who painted it?
- When was it created?
- What does it depict?

OPINIONS
- What do you like/dislike about it?
- Why is it famous?
- What might others see when they look at it?

RATINGS
On a scale of 1-5, rate the following:
- Technique
- Visual appeal
- Style/color
- Popularity

EVALUATION
Now, give your evaluation based on your answers above. Which painting is "better"? Why? Write your answers on the back or on a separate sheet of paper. Be prepared to discuss.

Handout I.4: Evaluative Thinking Avatar

Name: _____

CREATE YOUR EVALUATIVE THINKING AVATAR.	DEVELOP CRITERIA
CONSIDER PERSPECTIVES	**ASSIGN VALUE**
DISCUSS GRAY AREAS	**MAKE AND DEFEND JUDGEMENTS**

TABLE I.1
Artwork Analysis Key Understandings

	Still Life with Flowers	Irises
Facts	❑ Still life painting of a variety of flowers in a vase ❑ Natural texture ❑ Subtle tones ❑ Very realistic, including shading, depth, and details present ❑ Symmetrical in nature ❑ Created in 1617 ❑ Most expensive painting by this artist sold for $4.6 million	❑ Still life painting of irises in a vase ❑ Passionate brush stroke with a thicker texture ❑ Bright, bold colors ❑ Slightly abstract in form, distinctive lines ❑ Asymmetrical in nature ❑ Created in 1890 ❑ Most expensive painting by this artist sold for $82.5 million
Opinions	❑ Famous for its attention to detail and delicacy of work ❑ Appeals to those who prefer darker color palettes	❑ Famous for being by a master impressionist painter ❑ Appeals to those who prefer bolder artwork
Ratings	❑ Students will rate based on their own assessment	❑ Students will rate based on their own assessment

- ■ Discussing Gray Area
- ■ Making and Defending Judgments
- ❑ As students complete each target learning skill, they will pause and reflect on the key details of each sub-skill. This is a time for the students to synthesize their learning and record the key ideas for each learning target. At the conclusion of each sub-skill, students will return to this page and illustrate their original avatar using their newly learned skill.
- ❑ Allow students time to illustrate their avatar (the outline in the top left box) to represent a convergent thinking character/avatar of their choice. The other five boxes will remain empty for now, being filled in as students complete each sub-skill in the unit.

Bibliography

Bosschaert, A. (1617). *Still life with flowers [painting]*. Netherlands: Rijksmuseum. https://artsandculture.google.com/asset/still-life-with-flowers-ambrosius-bosschaert-the-elder/UgGmKyl0WuuDEA?hl=en.

van Gogh, V. (1890). *Irises [painting]*. New York: The Met. https://www.metmuseum.org/art/collection/search/436528.

CHAPTER 1

Sub-Skill 1

Considering Perspectives

TABLE 1.1
Considering Perspectives Sub-Skill Outline

	Thinking Skill Outline
Focus Questions	❑ How do we see things? How do others see them? ❑ What happens when others' ideas differ? ❑ What perspectives are important to consider? ❑ How do we define things differently? The same way?
Lesson 1	*Understanding Viewpoints* ❑ **Trade Book Focus:** *Who Is the Beast?* by Keith Baker ❑ **Practice Activity:** What's the Issue? Students will consider a variety of scenarios from various viewpoints to investigate how unique perspectives affect our approaches.
Lesson 2	*How Personal Viewpoints Affect Others* ❑ **Trade Book Focus:** *Tidy* by Emily Gravett ❑ **Practice Activity:** Circle of Viewpoints: Students interview various people about a topic, creating a circle of viewpoints to consider and discuss.
Authentic Application Activity	*Merging Viewpoints* ❑ **Practice Activity:** Recipe for a Good Day: Students create recipes for "good days" from their own perspective, and then as a group, merge their viewpoints into key ideas that are necessary for a good day.

DOI: 10.4324/9781003268352-2

EVALUATIVE THINKING for Advanced Learners, Grades 3–5

Considering Perspectives Lesson 1: Understanding Viewpoints

Objective: Develop an understanding of the idea that individuals have unique and varied perspectives.

Materials

- ❏ Handout 1.1: Considering Perspectives Anchor Chart (one for display)
- ❏ *Who Is the Beast?* by Keith Baker (teacher's copy)
- ❏ Handout 1.2: Read Aloud Reflection (one per student)
- ❏ Figure 1.1 (projected via document camera or enlarged to display)
  - ■ Also available online at: https://unsplash.com/photos/qlOsBqqw1AU
- ❏ Figure 1.2 (projected via document camera or enlarged to display)
  - ■ Also available online at: https://unsplash.com/photos/FA8HEWO9Vd8
- ❏ Figure 1.3 (projected via document camera or enlarged to display)
  - ■ Also available online at: https://unsplash.com/photos/7G_5KUKYqtk
- ❏ Figure 1.4 (projected via document camera or enlarged to display)
  - ■ Also available online at: https://unsplash.com/photos/SPjqx18O-Hg
- ❏ Handout 1.3: What's the Issue? Student Page (one per student)
- ❏ Handout 1.4: What's the Issue? Perspective Cards (duplicated as needed so that each student will receive one perspective per image)

Whole Group Introduction

- ❏ Tell students that today they will be learning about perspectives. Each person has a unique perspective, based upon their experiences (schema) and desires. Tell students:
  - ■ Let's start by thinking together. I'd like to see if we can all share thoughts, so let's think about the same thing at the same time.
  - ■ Everyone think about a chair. Imagine that chair, noticing color, feel, size, and where it is located. Turn and tell a partner about that chair. How did your thoughts compare?

Handout 1.1: Considering Perspectives Anchor Chart

CONSIDERING PERSPECTIVES

THINKING ABOUT PROBLEMS FROM MANY ANGLES

- Now, let's think about a cat. Take a moment, close your eyes, and everyone imagine a cat. Now, open your eyes. Turn and tell your partner about the cat. How did your thoughts compare?
- ❏ Discuss: What did students notice about trying to all think the same thought? Were we all thinking about the same thing? How do we know?

Read Aloud Activity

- ❏ Ask students: What comes to mind when you think of a beast? Why?
- ❏ Tell them that today you will read a story about a beast. Ask them to think as you read about who the beast could be.
- ❏ Read aloud *Who Is the Beast?* by Keith Baker. Pause on each page to allow students to make observations.
- ❏ At the end, discuss: Who was the beast really? How do you know?
- ❏ Distribute the Read Aloud Reflection page (Handout 1.2). Guide students as they think through the reflective questions on this page. Key understandings for the read aloud are outlined in Box 1.1. Allow students to talk in pairs or small groups about the pictures they create on this page before they complete the final question.

Box 1.1: *Who Is the Beast?* Key Understandings

- ❏ *Story summary*: A tiger wanders through the jungle overhearing other animals talking about and describing a "beast." The tiger wonders who the beast could be. As he wanders back through the jungle, he discovers that he shares many traits with other animals, leaving him wondering, "Who is the beast?"
- ❏ *Connection to perspectives*: This book shows that we all see things in our own way. Each animal describes a trait of the tiger, calling him the beast, but the tiger does not see himself as a beast. Instead, he notes all the traits he shares with other animals.

Handout 1.2: Read Aloud Reflection
Who is the Beast? by Keith Baker

Name: _____

Summarize the main idea of the story.	How did the book show perspectives?

In each box, draw what comes to mind when you think of the descriptor. Be ready to share your thoughts!		
RED	COLD	WET

How were your ideas similar to/different from your classmates? Why do you think this is the case?

Skill Development Activity

- Tell students that a big part of evaluative thinking is determining where the actual problem/challenge/issue lies. In this activity, students will be given a specific role to embody and asked to consider an image from that particular perspective. They'll need to think through their role's motivations, values, and desires in order to find the main "issue" in each image.
- Define "issue" as something that could be a challenge to overcome. For example, if it suddenly started raining outside and I forgot my umbrella, my main issue would be how to stay dry when I need to leave school.
- Remind students that depending on their unique perspective, the issue could be different than what others see as the main problem. This is the core understanding in this activity.
- Prepare the Perspective Cards (Handout 1.4). Cut apart the four perspectives for each picture. Then, distribute one perspective/value card to each student for each picture. They will glue it into the correct space on their response sheet. Multiple students may end up with the same perspective; it will encourage discussion to have several students working with various perspectives.
- Distribute Handout 1.3. Introduce the activity by telling students that they will be considering a variety of images today. They'll have to place themselves in someone else's shoes and think about what each unique perspective might focus on in a given situation.
- Display Figure 1.1. Ask students to share what they observe, guiding them to understand the context of the picture if they're not sure. Allow a few moments for sharing of general observations.
- Distribute role/value cards from Handout 1.4 for Figure 1.1: Boardwalk. There are four unique perspectives, and each student will be randomly assigned to one based on distribution (make enough so that each student has one, even if multiple students have similar perspectives). Students will glue this card to their recording sheet (Handout 1.3) in the first row.
- Ask students to think about the main issue shown in this image through the lens of their unique perspective. To scaffold for higher student support, allow partners or teams with the same perspectives to discuss and work together. See Table 1.2 for examples of possible "issues" that could be seen from each perspective.
- Once all students have determined a central issue and recorded it on their page, share as a larger group. Discuss various perspectives and why they differ. Also draw attention to how these perspectives interact.
- Repeat the activity again with Figure 1.2 (Rainy Day in the City), Figure 1.3 (Child Eating Ice Cream), and Figure 1.4 (Day at the Beach).
- Conclude the activity with a short discussion of how unique perspectives can change the focus in a situation.

Figure 1.1 *Hot Dog Stand on the Boardwalk.* A crowd of people in front of a hot dog stand on a boardwalk

Figure 1.2 *A Rainy Day in the City.* A city street with cars and people walking on the sidewalk in the rain

Figure 1.3 *A Child Eating an Ice Cream Cone.* A child holding a small ice cream cone

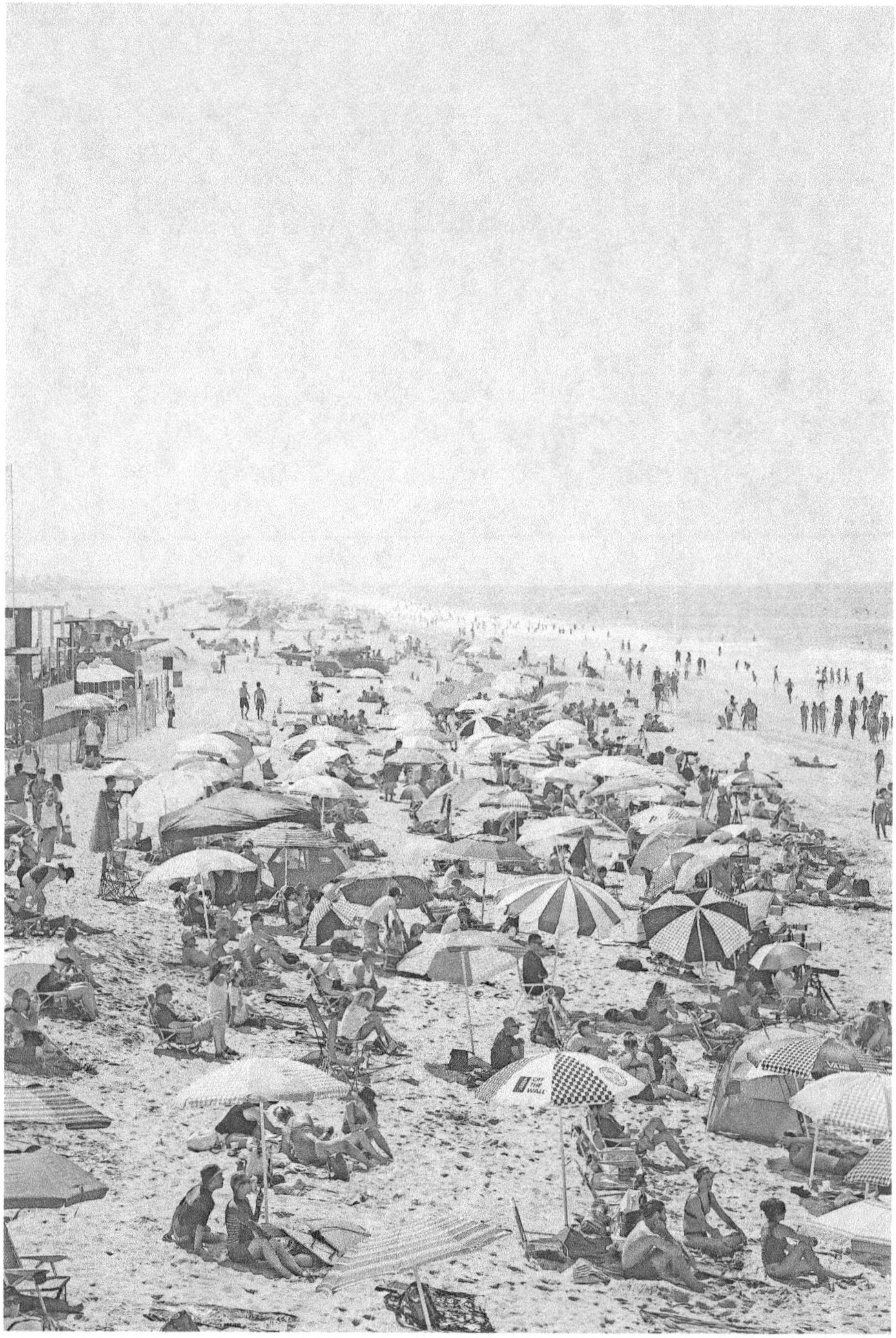

Figure 1.4 *A Day at a Crowded Beach.* A crowded beach with people

Handout 1.3: What's the Issue?

Name: _____

Look at each picture. For each image, your teacher will give you a card with a unique perspective. Observe the picture through the lens of your given perspective to determine what you think is the MAIN problem or issue.

perspective	values	In this column, state what you feel the MAIN problem or issue is, based on your unique perspective.
	GLUE ROLE / VALUE CARDS HERE	

Describe this activity. Were some perspectives trickier than others? Why is it important to recognize that others may see a problem differently (or not at all)?

Handout 1.4: What's the Issue? Perspective Cards

Cut apart the four perspectives for each picture. Then, distribute one perspective/value card to each student for each picture. They will glue it into the correct space on their response sheet.

Image 1.1: Boardwalk

MANAGER OF THE HOT DOG STAND
Your goal is to sell as many hot dogs as you can while still keeping quality high. You need to sell hot dogs to be able to make money!

MANAGER OF A NEARBY PIZZA SELLER
Your pizza stand is close to the Nathan's hot dog stand, and you compete for customers. You need to sell pizza to make money!

HUNGRY PERSON
You're walking the board walk and need to eat—soon! You're craving a hot dog.

BOARDWALK CUSTODIAN
Your job is to keep the boardwalk area neat, clean, and free of litter. You take great pride in your work, and you're very good at it!

Image 1.2: City Rain

METEOROLOGIST
Your job is to predict the weather. People count on you to be accurate so that they can plan their clothing and activities each day!

CAB DRIVER
You work to get people around the city. You need to get them to their destinations as quickly and safely as possible.

PEDESTRIAN
You are walking the city to get to your destination. You need to be careful, and arrive as quickly as possible while staying dry!

COMMUTOR
You are on your way to work and need to get there as quickly and safely as possible.

Handout 1.4, cont.: What's the Issue? Perspective Cards

Cut apart the four perspectives for each picture. Then, distribute one perspective/value card to each student for each picture. They will glue it into the correct space on their response sheet.

Image 1.3: Ice Cream

PERSON WHO WILL DO THE LAUNDRY	You are in charge of doing this child's laundry. It's important the clothes are clean and not stained.
KID EATING ICE CREAM	You love ice cream and have a cone of your favorite flavor. Of course you want to enjoy every bite!
ICE CREAM SELLER	You need to sell ice cream and toppings to stay in business. The more scoops and toppings you can sell, the better!
PARENT OF THE CHILD	You bought your child an ice cream cone. You know it might get messy, and you have to go somewhere important later.

Image 1.4: Beach Day

LIFEGUARD	Your job is to keep an eye on the people to make sure that everyone is safe. You have to keep a close eye on the whole beach and all the people there.
ENVIRONMENTAL ACTIVIST	You work to save natural spaces and habitats, including beaches. You want to make sure humans don't negatively impact nature.
DERMATOLOGIST	You are a doctor who specializes in skin health. You work hard to educate people about sunscreen and the dangers of too much sun exposure.
VACATIONER	You have come to the beach for a relaxing few days of vacation. You can't wait to relax with a good book and put your toes in the sand!

TABLE 1.2

What's the Issue? Sample Issues

	Perspective	Potential "Issues"
Figure 1.1: Boardwalk	Manager of the Hot Dog Stand	❏ Ensuring supply keeps up with demand ❏ Ensuring quality customer service ❏ Food quality
	Manager of a Nearby Pizza Seller	❏ Competing with the hot dog stand for customers ❏ Speed of service (faster service may mean more customers) ❏ Food quality
	Hungry Person	❏ Length of line/wait time ❏ Food quality ❏ Availability of choices
	Boardwalk Custodian	❏ Making sure people use available trash bins ❏ Emptying trash bins ❏ Sanitation/cleaning tables
Figure 1.2: City Rain	Meteorologist	❏ Getting the forecast right ❏ Predicting how long the weather will last ❏ Keeping an eye out for severe storms
	Cab Driver	❏ Road safety ❏ Additional rides/fares due to rain ❏ Traffic and parking with increased traffic
	Pedestrian	❏ Staying dry ❏ Finding a different travel plan (cab/subway) ❏ Making sure you have an umbrella
	Commuter	❏ Staying dry on the way to work ❏ Finding the fastest route to be on time ❏ Having an umbrella and/or rain boots
Figure 1.3 Ice Cream	Person Who Will Do the Laundry	❏ How to remove ice cream stains ❏ Getting extra mess off the shirt ❏ Ensuring that the child has a change of clothes if these get messy
	Kid Eating Ice Cream	❏ If the flavor is one you like ❏ Making sure the scoop stays on the cone ❏ Eating the treat before it melts
	Ice Cream Seller	❏ Making sure you have plenty of supply ❏ Trying to sell additional scoops ❏ Keeping a good supply of toppings
	Parent of the Child	❏ Trying to contain the messiness of the ice cream ❏ Having wipes or napkins on hand to clean up ❏ Making sure the ice cream is finished before the appointment time

(Continued)

TABLE 1.2
(Continued)

	Perspective	Potential "Issues"
Figure 1.4 Beach Day	Lifeguard	❏ Being able to see all the swimmers on a crowded beach ❏ Making sure that parents are watching their children ❏ Making sure that the water is safe for swimming
	Environmental Activist	❏ Keeping people from littering on beaches ❏ Ensuring that wildlife aren't pushed from their habitats ❏ Making sure that the people using the beach are taking care of the space
	Dermatologist	❏ Making sure people use sunscreen ❏ Finding shady spots to get out of the sun ❏ Thinking about how much time people have spent in the sun
	Vacationer	❏ Finding a good spot to set up ❏ Having space that's not too crowded ❏ Making sure you have all the supplies you need

Considering Perspectives Lesson 2: How Personal Viewpoints Affect Others

Objective: Develop an understanding of how personal viewpoints may affect others.

Materials

- ❏ *Tidy* by Emily Gravett (teacher's copy)
- ❏ Handout 1.5: Read Aloud Reflection
- ❏ Technology to display the animated short "Bear Rules"
  - ■ https://www.nfb.ca/playlists/learning-through-empathy-elementary/playback/#1
- ❏ Handout 1.6: Circle of Viewpoints

Whole Group Introduction

- ❏ Remind students that everyone has a unique viewpoint. Viewpoints are valid, and each person's perspective is made up of their own schema and desires.

- ❏ Choose or elicit three student volunteers to come to the front. Tell the volunteers: "I know how much you love recess. Today, I would like to give just the three of you an additional 10 minutes of recess. Would you like that? The only thing is, that in order for you to get this extra recess, you'll need to be supervised. I will go outside with you to supervise, but that means the rest of the class must sit inside and complete a worksheet while a substitute watches them."
- ❏ Engage students in a discussion, asking how they feel, and what desires are conflicting. Some students may want the extra playtime, but that negatively affects the others. What perspectives must we consider before we can have our wants met?

Read Aloud Activity

- ❏ Tell students that today you'll be reading a story about a character who has a very distinct perspective. Ask them to be on the lookout for how that character follows his own viewpoint, and what effect that has on others.
- ❏ Read aloud *Tidy*. Pause to think aloud about how the badger's perspective that things should be tidy affects other forest animals.
- ❏ Complete the Read Aloud Reflection (Handout 1.5), discussing cause-and-effect relationships that originate from personal perspectives. See Box 1.2 for key understandings to target.

Box 1.2: *Tidy* Key Understandings

- ❏ *Story summary*: In this story, Pete the badger thinks things should be tidy. He travels around the forest, tidying up everything, and in the process clears out the habitats of his fellow forest animals. When he realizes how his tidying has affected others, he helps the other animals rebuild their forest, vowing to think about how his actions affect others in the future.
- ❏ *Connection to perspectives*: Pete realizes through the course of this story that his unique perspective is not shared by others. Following through on his own ideas without thinking about the perspectives/needs of others leads to conflict and the destruction of the forest.

Handout 1.5: Read Aloud Reflection
Tidy by Emily Gravett

Name: _____

| Summarize the main idea of the story. | How did the book show perspective? |

Think about cause-and-effect relationships in the story. How do Pete's perspectives and actions affect those around him? How do others have an impact on Pete? Describe three of these relationships below.

Cause: → SO → Effect:

Cause: ← because ← Effect:

Cause: → SO → Effect:

❑ *Cause and effect*: There are many examples of cause and effect; for example:
  ■ Pete rakes up all the fall leaves in the forest, which causes him to notice that the trees look bare and scrappy. The trees look bare and scrappy, so Pete digs them up.
  ■ There is a flood, which causes mud. This leads Pete to bring in construction equipment and pave over the forest.
  ■ Pete is unable to find food or the door to his burrow because he has paved over the forest floor.
  ■ Pete spends a lonely, hungry, cold night on the pavement, which causes him to realize that he took his tidying too far. The next morning, he rebuilds the forest.

Skill Development Activity

❑ Tell students that you'll be watching a short clip three times. Each time, they'll watch with a different mindset/lens. This clip depicts an explorer coming to a new land, and how the native inhabitant responds. Distribute the Circle of Viewpoints page (Handout 1.6).
❑ Show the video clip "Bear Rules" one time. As soon as it finishes, have students summarize the clip as subjectively as possible in the center circle of their worksheet. This should sound like a news report, simply stating facts and giving an overall impression of the events.
❑ For the second viewing, students will put on the mindset of the native inhabitant. They should carefully watch the native, noting his reactions. Placing themselves in his shoes, they should describe the events from the native's point of view in the corresponding section on their Circle of Viewpoints.
  ■ **Key Understanding:** Students should recognize that the native inhabitant does not understand why the stranger has come to his home. He has clearly lived in this place for a long time and is used to the conditions; he does not have sympathy for the newcomer's challenges here.
❑ Show the clip a third time, this time asking students to work from the explorer's point of view. Repeat the process of recording the events from the explorer's point of view on the Circle of Viewpoints.
  ■ **Key Understanding:** The explorer clearly has a big ego—he thinks that he can claim any land he lands on. Even though he has challenges, he is determined to claim this new land for himself.

Handout 1.6: Circle of Viewpoints

Name: _____

Watch the short video: "The Bear Facts". In the center circle, summarize the clip, keeping your summary as objective as possible. Then, consider the viewpoints of the two characters in the video, as well as your own thoughts on what happens in the clip.

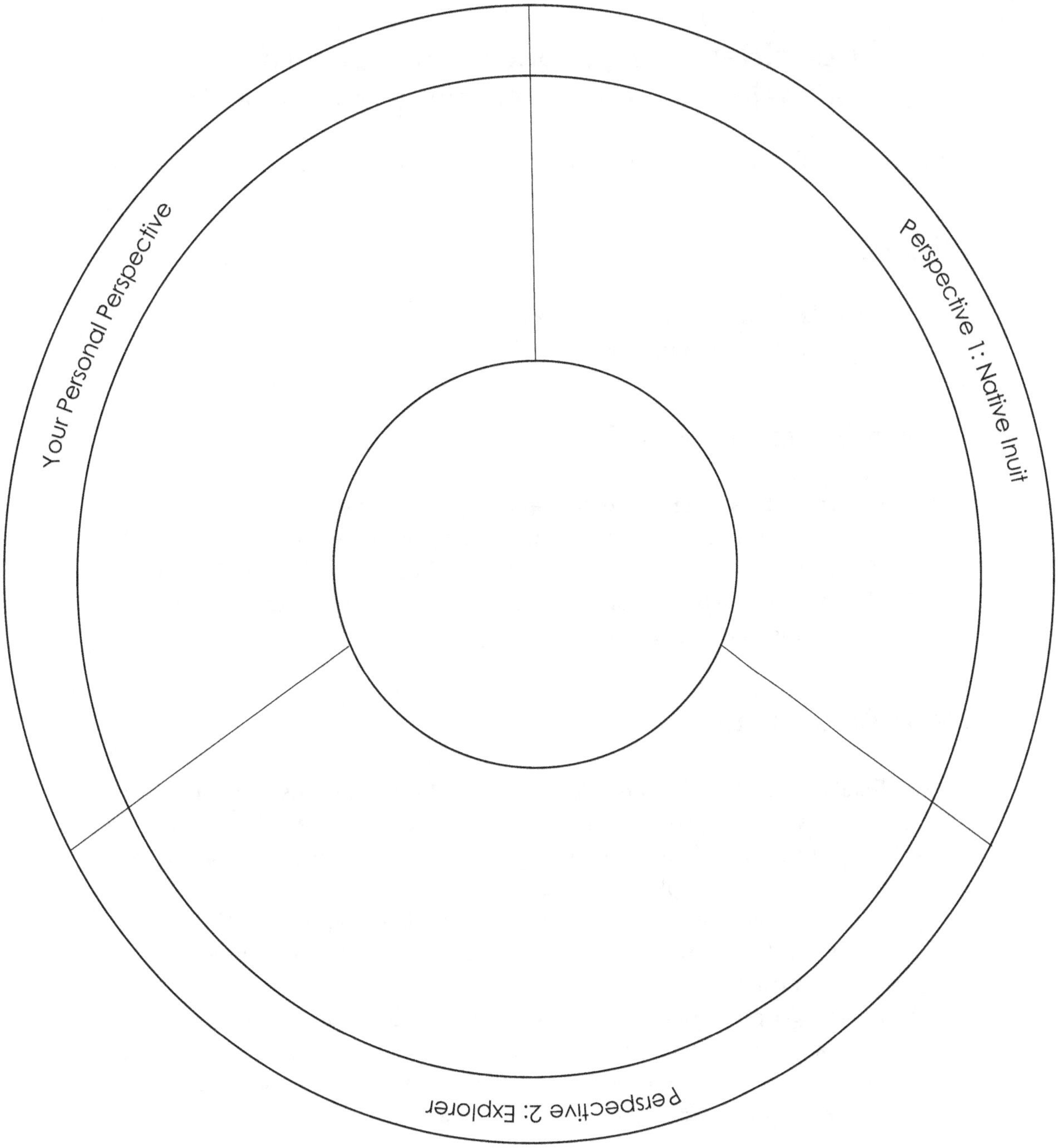

- Your Personal Perspective
- Perspective 1: Native Inuit
- Perspective 2: Explorer

- ❏ Discuss: What was different? How did your mindset change by placing yourselves in different perspectives?
- ❏ After a brief group discussion, have students write their own viewpoint on the events (objective, including their feelings/opinions) in the corresponding section of their Circle of Viewpoints. Follow up with a turn-and-talk or brief whole group sharing session for closure.

Considering Perspectives Authentic Application Activity: Merging Viewpoints

Objective: Apply the idea of personal perspective to an authentic context.

Materials

- ❏ *Daniel's Good Day* by Micha Archer
- ❏ Handout 1.7: A Good Day

Whole Group Introduction

- ❏ Review with students the concept of perspectives. Remind students that perspectives are unique to individuals; each person has their own!
- ❏ Review the Considering Perspectives Anchor Chart (Handout 1.1) and elicit student responses as to the most important things they've learned about considering perspectives.

Read Aloud Activity

- ❏ Read Aloud *Daniel's Good Day* by Micha Archer. In this story, a young boy asks several people what makes a good day for them. Take time to pause and think aloud as you read, considering the various perspectives of the different people Daniel speaks to.
- ❏ After reading, ask students to consider which character(s) they most relate to. Discuss what made a good day for the various characters, as well as Daniel.
- ❏ Be sure to point out that each character's "good day" was unique to them and based on their own perspective; what worked for one person might not work for another. In the same vein, be sure to note that each person's good day did not interfere with another's.

Handout 1.7: A Good Day

Name: _____

You have a whole day (10 hours) to fill. How do you make sure it's a good day? Use the chart below to section off your time. How do you spend your hours? Some activities may take more than an hour, some may take less. Color code your day to show how you'll spend your ten hours during your good day.

> Interview several classmates. What do others have in common with your good day?

> What things are unique to your own perspective of a good day?

> As a group, what elements seem necessary for your class to have a good day *together*? (think about things that many classmates had in common)

EVALUATIVE THINKING for Advanced Learners, Grades 3–5

Authentic Application Activity

- Distribute the A Good Day worksheet (Handout 1.7). Tell students that they will have a "Good Day" to fill. They will be given 10 hours to work with and will plan out their day. The table on the sheet is broken into 10 segments, each representing 1 hour. Some activities students choose may take more than 1 hour, some may take less; they should divide their day accordingly.
- Before students go too crazy, place a few constraints on their day:
  1. They cannot spend more than $100 on their day (no unlimited shopping sprees).
  2. They need to stay close to home/community (they can't fly to the moon).
  3. At least one activity should include others (they can't stay in their room and play video games for 10 hours).
  4. They should include at least one meal.
  5. Their good day should not cause anyone else to have a bad day (their day should affect others as minimally as possible).
- Allow students some time to work. Encourage them to color their time segments, using a different color for each distinct activity.
- Share good days. Students may share with partners or small groups, or you may choose to share out as a whole group.
- Once students have shared their plans for their days, they should complete the reflection questions at the bottom of the page.
- As an optional extension, encourage students to write creatively, crafting a fictional journal entry about their good day. Allow time for students to illustrate their stories and display them if possible.

Considering Perspectives Concluding Activities

- Distribute the Considering Perspectives Exit Ticket (Appendix A). Ask students to reflect on their learning about considering the perspectives of others and thinking through how unique perspectives might affect others. Allow time for students to complete the exit ticket. Use this as a formative assessment to gain a better understanding of your students' readiness to effectively practice the skill.
- If desired, complete the Group Using Considering Perspectives (Appendix A) to track students' progress with the skill.
- If desired, use the Evaluative Thinking Student Observation Rubric (Appendix A) to assess and quantify individual students' mastery.

❏ Ask students to retrieve their Evaluative Thinking Avatar (Handout I.4). In the Considering Perspectives box, they should either record the main ideas about the thinking skill or illustrate their avatar using the skill of Considering Perspectives.

Bibliography

Archer, M. (2019). *Daniel's good day.* New York: Penguin Random House.
Baker, K. (1990). *Who is the beast?* Chicago, IL: HMH Books.
Beach day. (n.d.). Photo by Josh Duke on Unsplash.
Boardwalk. (n.d.). Photo by Thomas Loizeau on Unsplash.
Child with ice cream. (n.d.). Photo by Mieke Campbell on Unsplash.
Gravett, E. (2017). *Tidy.* Hampshire, UK. Pan Macmillan.
Rain in the City. (n.d.). Photo by Luke Stackpoole on Unsplash.
Wright, J. (Animator short film). (2010). *Bear rules.* [Animated Short Film]. National Film Board of Canada. https://www.nfb.ca/playlists/learning-through-empathy-elementary/playback/#1.

CHAPTER 2

Sub-Skill 2

Developing Criteria

TABLE 2.1
Developing Criteria Sub-Skill Overview

Focus Questions	❏ What matters? How do you know? ❏ What is the foundation for your reasoning? ❏ What must we consider as we choose?
Lesson 1	*Personal Considerations* ❏ **Trade Book Focus:** *Ira Sleeps Over* by Bernard Waber ❏ **Practice Activity:** Must/Might: Students consider what is essential to each given scenario.
Lesson 2	*External Considerations* ❏ **Trade Book Focus:** *Stellaluna* by Janell Cannon ❏ **Practice Activity:** What is the best fit? Students consider the "best fit" elements of groups and provide their criteria for reasoning.
Authentic Application Activity	*Formulating Your Own Criteria* ❏ **Trade Book Focus:** *If I Built a House* by Chris Van Dusen ❏ **Authentic Application:** Students develop criteria and a "must have/could have" list to design their dream house which will also meet the needs of their family.

Developing Criteria Lesson 1: Personal Considerations

Objective: Develop an understanding of what criteria are and how they factor into the decision-making process.

Materials

- Handout 2.1: Personal Considerations Anchor Chart (one for display)
- *Ira Sleeps Over* by Bernard Waber (teacher's copy)
- Handout 2.2: Read Aloud Reflection (one per student)
- Handout 2.3: Must/Might Worksheet (one per student)

Whole Group Introduction

- Tell students that today you'll be discussing what it means to develop criteria. Show the Developing Criteria Anchor Chart (Handout 2.1).
- Tell students that the word *criteria* refers to things we must consider when we make a choice. Pose at least one of the following questions:
  - If I wanted to climb Mount Everest, what would I need to consider?
  - If I wanted to go scuba diving, what would I need to consider?
  - If I want to make sure I can get into my top choice college, what do I need to consider?
  - If I want to become a [insert career] when I grow up, what do I need to consider?

Read Aloud Activity

- Circle back with students, reminding them that every choice or goal has criteria (considerations) that we must think about. Tell them that you'll be reading a book today in which a boy must think through a tough choice. As you read, ask students to look for criteria that Ira considers about whether or not to take his bear with him to the sleepover.
- Read *Ira Sleeps Over*. As you read, point out considerations for Ira (input of others, awareness of social norms, etc.).
- After reading, distribute the Read Aloud Reflection (Handout 2.2). Allow students some time to reflect, and then gather the whole group back together and discuss: What were the most important criteria for

Handout 2.1: Developing Criteria Anchor Chart

DEVELOPING CRITERIA

DETERMINING WHAT IS IMPORTANT

Handout 2.2: Read Aloud Reflection
Ira Sleeps Over by Bernard Waber

Name: _____

| Summarize the main idea of the story. | What criteria did Ira have to consider? |

1 What are three perspectives Ira considers in the story?

2 What effect does each perspective have on Ira's decision to take (or not take) his bear to Reggie's house?

What do you think is (or should be) the <u>most important</u> consideration for Ira?

Ira? How do you know? Key understandings for this read aloud are outlined in Box 2.1.

> ## Box 2.1: *Ira Sleeps Over* Key Understandings
>
> ❏ *Story summary*: A young boy is invited to sleep over at a friend's house. He can't decide whether or not he should bring his teddy bear with him, and seeks the advice of his family. In the end, he decides that what is most important to him is having his bear with him no matter what anyone else thinks.
> ❏ *Connection to criteria*: Ira considers the advice (considerations) of others, but what is important to others is not necessarily indicative of what is best for Ira.
> ❏ *Various perspectives considered*:
> ■ Ira's sister thinks that his friend will find the teddy bear baby-ish.
> ■ Ira's parents encourage him to take the bear.
> ■ Reggie won't talk to Ira about teddy bears; later we discover that Reggie had hidden his own bear from Ira.

Skill Development Activity

❏ Distribute the Must/Might sheet (Handout 2.3) to students. Tell them that for each activity we want to do, we must consider what is most necessary. Model the first activity, "Baking a Cake." Circle the "musts" (things that are essential to the activity), underline the "mights" (things that are optional, but might be nice to have/do), and cross out the "don't needs." Invite discussion; there may be some debate, especially between the "musts" and the "mights." Encourage students to back up their thinking with reasoning and evidence. After working through the existing items, help students to think of at least one more "must" and/or "might" for the activity.
❏ Invite students to complete the rest of the sheet either independently or with a partner. Circulate to discuss and ask probing questions. The final slot on the sheet asks students to create a "must"/"might"/"not needed" list for an activity of their own!
❏ Share and discuss as a group.

Handout 2.3: Must/Might Choices

Name: _____

Consider each of the following activities. Then, circle the tasks that are "musts" for the activity. Underline the tasks that are "mights", and cross out the tasks that are "not needed". Then, think: is there anything else that's a "must do" or "could do" for that task?

Activity	(Must) //	<u>Might</u> //	~~Not Needed~~	What Else?
Baking a cake	oven chocolate broccoli spatula	bowl recipe eggs flour	icing sugar hammer cake mix	
Washing a car	sponge soap car hose	vacuum towel bucket binoculars	instructions snacks music scrub brush	
Building a bird house	wood bird seed hammer paint	drill computer crackers saw	instructions tree nails safety goggles	
Writing a story	paper computer pencil markers	ideas snacks desk playing cards	pen calculator title illustrations	
Your choice:				

DISCUSS: How did your selections compare with others'? What did you base your choices on?

Developing Criteria Lesson 2: External Considerations

Objective: Analyze how criteria can help us organize our thinking about the world.

Materials

- *Stellaluna* by Janell Cannon (teacher's copy)
- Handout 2.4: Read Aloud Reflection (one per student)
- Handout 2.5: Best Fits Worksheet (one per student)

Whole Group Introduction

- Remind students that criteria are considerations that we must think about as we make decisions. Sometimes, like in *Ira Sleeps Over*, we weigh these considerations in order to choose. Other times, these criteria are set, and help us to better understand our world.
- Think back to the previous activity, Must/Might. Ask: How did we know when something was essential (a must) for an activity? Discuss. Encourage the understanding that sometimes we have essential criteria. Knowing what these essential criteria are can help us arrive at solutions.

Read Aloud Activity

- Introduce the book *Stellaluna* by Janell Cannon. Tell students that this book is about a small bat who gets confused about what she is. Tell students that as you read, they should look for criteria that will help identify Stellaluna as what she really is—a bat.
- Read aloud *Stellaluna*. Model your thinking when you see criteria that alert students to distinguishing animals.
- After reading, ask: What was the main problem here? How did criteria help us get to the solution?
- Distribute the Read Aloud Reflection page (Handout 2.4) and allow students time to record their thinking. Key understandings are detailed in Box 2.2. If time allows, invite some sharing about the concepts on the reflection page.

Handout 2.4: Read Aloud Reflection
Stellaluna by Janell Cannon

Name: _____

| Summarize the main idea of the story. | How does Stellaluna decide what kind of animal she must be? |

Compare and contrast bats and birds.

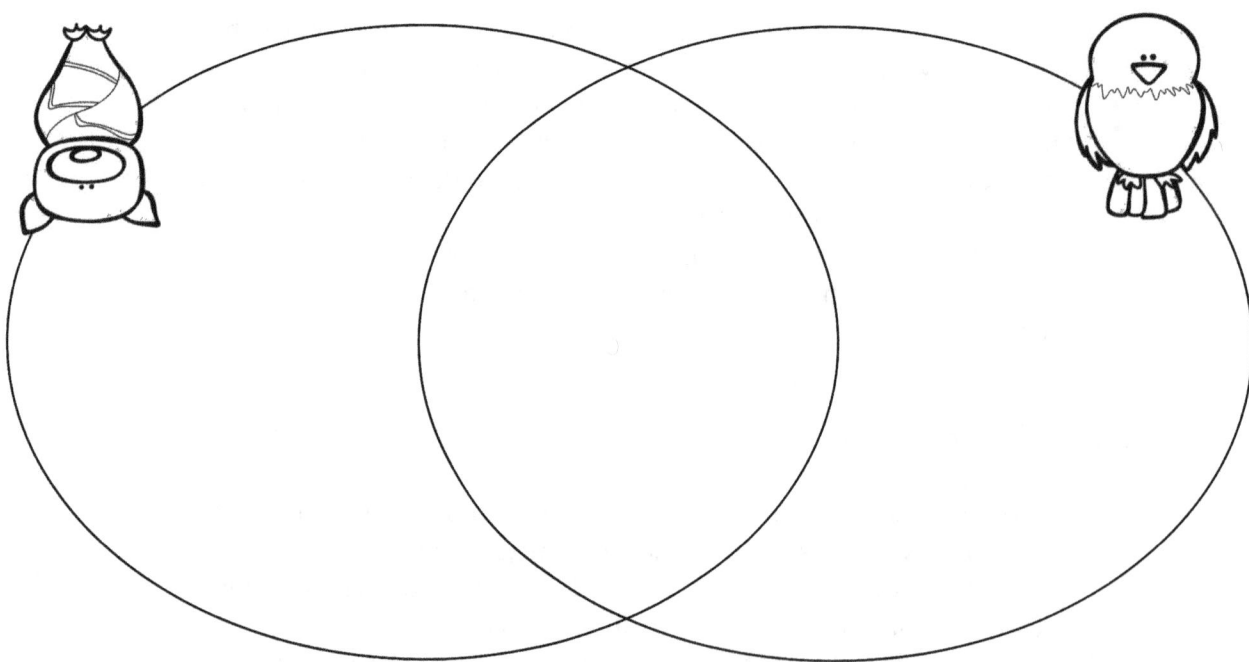

What are the most important criteria to define bats? Birds? Explain.

Box 2.2: *Stellaluna* Key Understandings

- *Story summary*: Stellaluna is a bat who gets separated from her family. She finds herself with a group of birds, and tries to ingratiate herself with them. Eventually, she finds that she does not fit in with the birds, but is, indeed, a bat.
- *Connection to criteria*: Stellaluna does not meet the criteria for being a bird. Although she tries to act like a bird (being active during the day, eating worms, hanging on branches by her claws/thumbs), when she finally meets with other bats, she is instinctually able to fit in again (being nocturnal, hanging upside-down, eating fruit).
- *Compare/contrast*: While birds and bats have many similarities (both fly, live in groups), bats are different in that they are nocturnal, hang on branches upside-down, have fur, and (in Stellaluna's case) eat fruit; birds eat worms and insects, are active during the day, have feathers, and sit upright on branches or in nests.
- *Most important criteria*: Any of the differences noted in the compare/contrast chart could be considered important criteria in defining bats and birds. Look for students to write a summative sentence defining each type of animal.

Skill Development Activity

- Distribute the Best Fits worksheet (Handout 2.5). Go through the directions with students carefully. They will look at the first column and develop their top criteria that make those things a "group." Then, they'll circle the object in the second column which fits their criteria and completes the group. Finally, they'll write their criteria in the third column.
- Allow students to work independently for several minutes on this activity. If they finish early, encourage them to complete the "Extend" activity at the bottom.
- After several minutes of independent time, allow students to discuss their answers in pairs or small groups. Encourage discussion about differing answers and criteria. As a whole group, discuss what makes something a correct answer. How do we know? Relate these criteria back to the read-aloud. What were the most important criteria for

SUPPORT MATERIAL

Handout 2.5: Best Fits

Name: _____

These things belong to a group.	Circle the ONE that also belongs to the group.	Describe why the things belong together.
 gull, goose, swan, duck	 bat, pelican, rooster, turtle	
 gumball, sucker, candy, Jell-O	 cupcake, orange, popcorn, yogurt	
 scissors, notebook, book, yellow crayon	 schoolbus, pen, eraser, teacher	

EXTEND: Create criteria for each object in the second column which could allow it to fit in with the group.
CHALLENGE: On the back, create your own grouping for a friend to solve!

Sub-Skill 2

TABLE 2.2

Best Fits Possible Solutions

These Things Belong in a Group	Circle One That Also Belongs	Potential "Best Fit" Connections
❏ Gull	❏ Bat	❏ BAT: has wings, can fly, one syllable
❏ Goose	❏ Pelican	❏ PELICAN: is a bird, lives near water, is white
❏ Swan	❏ Rooster	❏ ROOSTER: is a bird
❏ Duck	❏ Turtle	❏ TURTLE: lays eggs, lives near water
❏ Gumball	❏ Cupcake	❏ CUPCAKE: dessert treat
❏ Sucker	❏ Orange	❏ ORANGE: fruit-flavored, round
❏ Candy	❏ Popcorn	❏ POPCORN: two syllables, snack
❏ Jell-O	❏ Yogurt	❏ YOGURT: fruit-flavored, snack food, two syllables
❏ Scissors	❏ Schoolbus	❏ SCHOOLBUS: school-related, has a double letter
❏ Notebook	❏ Pen	❏ PEN: used with paper, school-related
❏ Book	❏ Eraser	❏ ERASER: used with paper, school-related
❏ Yellow Crayon	❏ Teacher	❏ TEACHER: found in a classroom, uses the supplies in the group

Stellaluna? Could we have more than one correct answer if we used different criteria? Why is this important to note as we solve problems?
❏ As you discuss, be sure to loop back and tie in the concept of perspectives: How do our perspectives/goals shape the criteria that are most important to us?
❏ As an optional extension, complete the Challenge activity, in which students create their own "best fit" puzzle for a partner to solve.

Developing Criteria Authentic Application Activity: Formulating Your Own Criteria

Objective: Combine both personal and external essential criteria into a new situation with an authentic context.

EVALUATIVE THINKING for Advanced Learners, Grades 3–5

Materials

- ❑ *If I Built a House* by Chris Van Dusen (teacher's copy)
- ❑ Handout 2.6: Dream House Planning and Presentation Pages (one per student)
- ❑ Optional: Art supplies for product publication

Whole Group Introduction

- ❑ Remind students of the concept of developing criteria. Important things to note are:
  - ■ Some criteria are *personal considerations* and apply only to specific people or situations. These are things that may be important for you, but not necessarily for others to be successful in a given situation. That these criteria are personal does not make them less important.
  - ■ Some criteria are *essential criteria* and would be important to a given situation or problem regardless of the audience. We can think of these as rules, such as "all reptiles are cold-blooded" or "schools need teachers to function."
- ❑ Review the Developing Criteria Anchor Chart (Handout 2.1) and elicit student responses as to the most important aspects/learnings about developing criteria.

Read Aloud Activity

- ❑ Introduce the book *If I Built a House* by Chris Van Dusen. In this story, a young boy imagines his dream house, and it becomes fairly fantastical!
- ❑ As you read, ask students to consider what the criteria were for the boy's dream house. He lets his imagination run wild—where are the constraints/considerations?
- ❑ Ask students: Was this dream house really practical? Why or why not? What else should the boy have considered?

Authentic Application Activity

- ❑ Distribute the My Dream House Planning and Product Page (Handout 2.6) to students. You may choose to distribute the planning

page first, and then the product page, or you may copy them front-to-back and hand the whole thing out at once.
- ❏ On the planning page, students will examine considerations and develop their must/might criteria for their dream house. Guide students in considering whether their criteria are essential (i.e., enough space for family members, inclusion of a kitchen and/or bathrooms), or personal (i.e., a backyard pool or a slide instead of stairs).
- ❏ Give students time to work. Circulate, helping students clarify and refine their criteria.
- ❏ Once students have determined their criteria, allow them to move to the next phase: drawing their dream.
- ❏ On the product page, students will illustrate their dream house, including labels for essential features.
- ❏ Once students have illustrated their dream houses, they should write a descriptive paragraph or essay about their dream house, including the criteria that went into planning. This can be done on a separate sheet of paper.
- ❏ Save some time for students to share their creations. Ask probing questions, such as:
  - ■ What did you have to consider? What were your most important criteria?
  - ■ How did you make sure that this house would work for your family?
  - ■ How did you incorporate both your "must haves" and your "could haves"?
  - ■ What is your favorite part of your house that doesn't necessarily go with your criteria, but was just for you?
  - ■ How are the houses different when we have different numbers of family members/pets?
- ❏ Remind students that both personal considerations as well as essential criteria informed their product.

Developing Criteria Concluding Activities

- ❏ Distribute the Developing Criteria Exit Ticket (Appendix A). Ask students to reflect on their learning about the skill of developing criteria that are relevant to a unique situation and effective in helping them think through potential solutions. Allow time for students to complete the exit ticket. Use this as a formative assessment to gain a better understanding of your students' readiness to effectively practice the skill.

Handout 2.6: My Dream House

Name: _____

You have the chance to build your dream house! First you need to consider the criteria you'll need. Fill in the table below to think about what kind of house you need to build.

Every house must have:	
Number of people in my family:	
Rooms we use every day:	
Activities we like to do:	
Pets we have:	
Other considerations:	

Now that you know what you must consider, use these criteria to develop a list of 'must have' and 'could have' items for your dream house.

MUST HAVE	COULD HAVE

Handout 2.6, continued: My Dream House

Name: _____

Draw a picture of your dream house. Use as much detail and color as possible. Consider labeling essential parts.

Share your house. Describe it using as much detail as possible! What did you have in common with others? What was different?

- ❏ If desired, complete the Group Using Developing Criteria (Appendix A) to track students' progress with the skill.
- ❏ If desired, use the Evaluative Thinking Student Observation Rubric (Appendix A) to assess and quantify individual students' mastery.
- ❏ Ask students to retrieve their Evaluative Thinking Avatar (Handout I.4). In the Developing Criteria box, they should either record the main ideas about the thinking skill or illustrate their avatar using the skill of Developing Criteria.

Bibliography

Cannon, J. (1993). *Stellaluna.* Boston, MA. Harcourt, Houghton Mifflin Harcourt.

Van Dusen, C. (2019). *If I built a house.* Westminster, London: Penguin Young Readers Group.

Waber, B. (1975). *Ira sleeps over.* Boston, MA. Houghton Mifflin Harcourt.

CHAPTER 3

Sub-Skill 3

Assigning Value

TABLE 3.1
Assigning Value Sub-Skill Outline

	Thinking Skill Outline
Focus Questions	❏ How can we determine what is important? ❏ What gives something value? ❏ Is value different based on different situations?
Lesson 1	*Identifying Importance* ❏ **Trade Book Focus:** *The Important Book* by Margaret Wise Brown ❏ **Practice Activity:** Writing Important Poems: Students choose an object to write about the most important things.
Lesson 2	*Orders of Importance* ❏ **Trade Book Focus:** *Inch by Inch* by Leo Lionni ❏ **Practice Activity:** Choose Two: students work to choose only two options from a set, determining which are the most valuable to the given situation.
Authentic Application Activity	*Writing the Rule Book* ❏ **Trade Book Focus:** *Tikki Tikki Tembo* by Arlene Mosel ❏ **Authentic Application:** Students create a rule book for the classroom, given only three rules to employ.

DOI: 10.4324/9781003268352-4

Assigning Value Lesson 1: Identifying Importance

Objective: Introduce the concept of assigning value by considering what is most important about an object/idea.

Materials

- ❏ Handout 3.1: Personal Considerations Anchor Chart (one for display)
- ❏ *The Important Book* by Margaret Wise Brown (teacher's copy)
- ❏ Handout 3.2: Read Aloud Reflection (one per student)
- ❏ Handout 3.3: An Important Poem (one per student)
- ❏ Optional: Art supplies for publishing poems

Whole Group Introduction

- ❏ Remind students that the purpose of developing criteria was to understand what was essential to solving a problem or interpreting a situation. In this thinking skill, students will be assigning value to those considerations, and determining what is more or less important.
- ❏ Share the Assigning Value Anchor Chart (Handout 3.1). Tell students that while criteria are important, we must also think about ranking what is more or less important. For an example, pose the following: "If I need to bake a cake, is it more important to have an oven, or an electric mixer?" While both components are used in cake baking, we cannot bake without an oven, so we would judge that the oven is more important than the mixer, even though they are both important.

Read Aloud Activity

- ❏ Share the cover of *The Important Book* by Margaret Wise Brown. In this book, the author shares what she considers to be most important about several common objects/ideas. Tell students to be on the lookout for general criteria for each object/idea, but also to see if they agree with what the author feels is most important about each.
- ❏ Read the book, pausing for a moment on each page to think about the criteria/most important aspects. As you read, don't allow students

Handout 3.1: Assigning Value Anchor Chart

ASSIGNING VALUE

DETERMINING WHAT IS MOST IMPORTANT

- to share their thoughts just yet; they'll do this on the Read Aloud Reflection page. This is tricky—you'll find students are eager to share areas where they disagree!
- ❏ Distribute the Read Aloud Reflection sheet (Handout 3.2). Invite students to independently work through the first two questions about the book. For key understandings to target, see Box 3.1. Then, ask them to turn and talk with a neighbor about their thinking. Ask for a few volunteers to share their thoughts. Summarize with the question: Why do you think the author chose those things as the *most* important?

> **Box 3.1: *The Important Book* Key Understanding**
>
> ❏ *Story summary*: The author communicates what she feels is "the most important thing" about a variety of topics in poem form. The first and last lines of each poem state the most important criteria, with additional criteria comprising the other lines of the poems.

Skill Development Activity

- ❏ After sharing their thoughts about the read aloud, students will each choose their own object/idea to consider. At the bottom of the Read Aloud Reflection page (Handout 3.2), students will complete a mind map to think about the essential criteria of their object/idea.
- ❏ Encourage students to be flexible in their thinking, adding more bubbles to the mind map if necessary. Help them to think about not only physical characteristics, but also emotions their object/idea evokes, uses for the object/idea, etc. Make heavy use of wait time as students complete their mind map.
- ❏ Once students have had ample time and opportunity to complete their mind map, they should use a highlighter to shade the bubble of the most important thing about their object/idea. Be sure students can explain to you what their criteria were for choosing this!
- ❏ Students will then work to publish their Important Poem on the publishing page (Handout 3.3). They should write their poem about their

Handout 3.2: Read Aloud Reflection
The Important Book by Margaret Wise Brown

Name: _____

| How did the author communicate what she felt was most important about each thing? | Do you agree with her ideas about what each "Important Thing" is? Explain. |

Now, choose an idea or object of your own. Create a mind map about all the characteristics of that object/idea. When you brainstorming characteristics, highlight the circle of the most important thing. If you need more 'bubbles', feel free to add them!

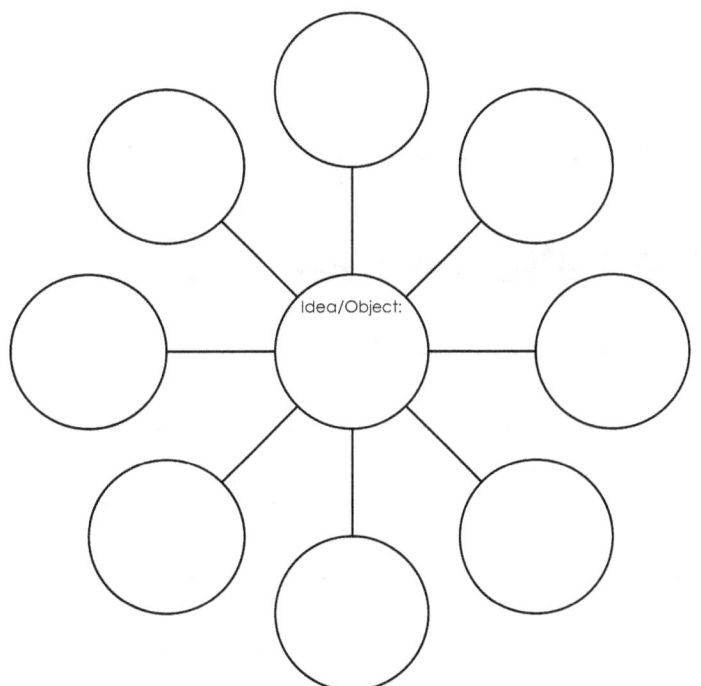

Handout 3.3: An Important Poem

Name: _____

Now, write an "Important" poem about the object/idea you mind mapped. Think about the most important thing! Use the style of *The Important Book* and be creative! Illustrate your poem in the space provided. Use the back if you need additional room.

The Important Thing About: _____

own object/idea in the style of *The Important Book*, inserting their own ideas/criteria. Students can illustrate their poems in the space at the top.
❏ Invite students to share their poems and discuss their thinking in choosing their most important criteria.

Assigning Value Lesson 2: Orders of Importance

Objective: Apply the concept of assigning value to determining orders of importance.

Materials

❏ *Inch by Inch* by Leo Lionni (teacher's copy)
❏ Handout 3.4: Food Chains Article (one per student)
❏ Handout 3.5: Read Aloud Reflection (one per student)
❏ Handout 3.6: Choose Two (one per student)

Whole Group Introduction

❏ Reflect on the previous lesson with students. Remind them that in the last lesson, they chose the single most important thing about an object or idea. In this lesson, they'll be looking at objects or ideas with many essential elements and ranking these elements in order of importance.
❏ Ask for volunteers to share the reasoning behind their choice for the most important thing in their poem writing. How did they determine that other criteria were less important?

Read Aloud Activity

❏ Tell students that they'll be looking for orders of importance in nature today. For this lesson, students will be reading an informational article as well as a picture book (fiction) and trying to assign value.
❏ Read aloud *Inch by Inch* by Leo Lionni. In this story, the birds do not see the importance of the inchworm, but the inchworm convinces them that he is, in fact, important. Stop at various points, thinking aloud about how the birds and other creatures judge the inchworm. Are they correct in their judgments?

- ❏ Then, distribute and share the informational article about food chains (Handout 3.4). This article connects to the story by linking the hierarchies that naturally occur in ecosystems.
- ❏ Distribute and complete the Read Aloud Reflection page (Handout 3.5), linking the story to the article and discussing how we can assign value to creatures who are all essential parts of an ecosystem. Key understandings for the read aloud can be found in Box 3.2.

> ### Box 3.2: *Inch By Inch*/Food Chains Key Understandings
>
> - ❏ *Story summary*: An inchworm offers to measure things for other animals in order to keep from being eaten. The other/larger animals do not always see the inchworm's value, but he proves himself useful.
> - ❏ *How animals assign value*: The animals assign value based on their own benefit. For example, the inchworm is only valuable as food for the robin until he offers to measure the robin's tail.
> - ❏ *Connections between the story and the article*: Each animal has an important role to play. Without any link in a food chain, there would be a ripple effect of consequences. The same is true in *Inch by Inch*, where each creature plays an important role.
> - ❏ *Food chain creation*: Answers here may vary, but one example would be: (1) grass, (2) inchworm, (3) robin, (4) snake, (5) hawk.
> - ❏ *Generalizations*: In general, each creature is of equal importance in that each creature has a role to play within its own ecosystem and food chain.

Skill Development Activity

- ❏ Point out to students that although we sometimes do assign value, or rank, to essential elements, it can often be tricky to do. Tell them that in this activity, they'll be considering three essential elements, but they'll only be allowed to "keep" two of them. Assign three areas of your classroom: Option A, Option B, and Option C. Clearly label these areas. Distribute the Choose Two Recording Sheet (Handout 3.6)
- ❏ Tell students that the first thing that you'll be thinking through will be "What makes a good friend?" Give students 30–60 seconds of silent

Handout 3.4: Food Chains

Name: _____

A **food chain** is a representation of the order in which animals rely on one another for food within an ecosystem. The food chain does not show every food source for each organism, rather, it gives an overview of the flow of energy from one organism to the next.

Most food chains begin with **producers**, or organisms that make their own food, like plants. After producers come **consumers**, or organisms that eat other organisms for energy. **Predators** eat animals lower in the food chain than themselves. **Prey** are eaten by the predators. Each consumer relies on another organism for food and energy. Once organisms die, they are broken down in the soil as nutrients for **decomposers**. Then, the food chain begins again as producers use these nutrients in the soil to grow and provide energy for consumers.

Many things can disrupt the food chain, like having too many predators in one area, or a lack of plants. When these disruptions happen, animals must look elsewhere for food sources.

Take a look at the food chains pictured to the right. What do you notice? Can you find the predators, prey, producers, or decomposers? How do you know where each organism ranks within the chain? Why is this important?

What other food chains are you familiar with? Share with a partner.

Handout 3.5: Read Aloud Reflection
Inch by Inch by Leo Lionni

Name: _____

Summarize the main idea of the story.	How did the animals assign value to one another?

Describe the connections you see between *Inch by Inch* and the article about food chains.

Based on the story and the article, create a food chain that includes both the inchworm and the robin. Label the ranks in the food chain from lowest (1) to highest (5).

Are some creatures more important than others? Write a generalization that includes evidence from both *Inch by Inch* as well as what you know about food chains.

Handout 3.6: Choose Two

Name: _____

Use this recording sheet to keep track of your choices as you play "Choose Two". Then, answer the reflection questions at the bottom.

Topic:			
Our three essential values:	1.	2.	3.
I chose to keep:		✚	Because…
Without _____, what would be different?			

Topic:			
Our three essential values:	1.	2.	3.
I chose to keep:		✚	Because…
Without _____, what would be different?			

What was the toughest choice for you? Why?	Which eliminated value do you think would have the biggest impact? Why?

EVALUATIVE THINKING for Advanced Learners, Grades 3–5

think time, and then elicit three responses. Ensure that each response is conceptually unique (for example, *kindness*, *honesty*, and *fun* are conceptually unique, while *kind*, *friendly*, and *nice* are conceptually similar). Record these three essential elements on the board where all can see them, and label them "Option A," "Option B," and "Option C." Tell students that while each of these options is great, they will only be allowed to keep two; the third they must live without.

- ❏ Give students a moment to think and to record both the concept "What makes a good friend?" as well as the essential characteristics on their Choose Two Recording Sheet. After a few moments of silent reflection, invite students to stand and move to the area that represents the option they would eliminate. Prompt discussion: Why did students choose what they did? Was there consensus among the options? What would the world be like without [Option *]?
- ❏ Invite students to record their choices and reflections on the recording sheet. Complete the activity again, using another concept, such as "a great meal," "a great teacher," "a superhero," or one of your choosing.
- ❏ Complete the reflection questions on the recording sheet.

Assigning Value Authentic Application Activity: Writing the Rule Book

Objective: Assign value to a real-world context, coming to consensus on what is most important when it comes to rules.

Materials

- ❏ *Tikki Tikki Tembo* by Arlene Mosel (teacher's copy)
- ❏ Handout 3.7: Rule Book Recording Sheet (one per student or small group)

Whole Group Introduction

- ❏ Revisit the concept of assigning value. Ask students to share their thoughts and learning. Clarify their thinking with questions such as the following:
  - ■ How do we know when something is important?
  - ■ How do our perspectives shape what we think is valuable?

- Is it possible for us to disagree about what is most important? Could we both be correct?
- How do criteria affect what we think is most important?

Read Aloud Activity

- Tell students that today you'll be sharing a story about a family who follows rules very carefully. These rules have been followed in all the traditions of their culture, and they stick to them. Ask students to consider as you read: What makes rules important to follow?
- Read aloud *Tikki Tikki Tembo* by Arlene Mosel. As you read, model your thinking, pausing at various points to ask questions like the following:
  - What is most important to the mother?
  - How can you tell the value of each child?
  - Are the values changing based on the experience with the well?
  - Why did they follow the rules so carefully even when it was harmful?
  - Was this rule (the naming rule) really the most important thing?

Authentic Application Activity

- Discuss with students the purpose of rules. As a whole group, create a T-chart about the concept of rules. Think about:
  - What makes rules valuable?
  - What are rules used for?
  - What are some examples of rules in our school? Classroom? Community?
- Tell students that they will be writing a rule book. Tell them that for this activity, they will be limited to three rules. Remind them to think through what makes a rule a good one, and also to think about why rules exist.
- Review your existing classroom rules. What is most important? What could be combined/eliminated? Is anything missing that would be important to include?
- Divide students into work teams. Teamwork for this activity will allow students to have some dialogue and debate amongst themselves, ultimately coming to a consensus. Allow students some time to work in teams to write a new rule book. Circulate to help teams work through debates.

Handout 3.7: Rule Book Recording Sheet

Name: _____

The important thing about RULES is:

Some of our current class rules are:

Some rules my team thinks are important are:

As a whole class, our three most important rules are:

Why do we need rules?

EXTEND: One example of a rule that's NOT a good one is:

- Allow student teams to present their three rules. Probe for reasoning about why each rule was chosen. Record rules as they are reported on the board, making a running list of all rules that are selected by teams. Be sure to record all responses, even if they are repeated.
- Once all teams have shared, ask the group to consider the class list. "Where were things repeated amongst groups? Does anything stand out? What generalizations can we make about our classroom rules?" Consider changing your list of class rules to reflect consensus from this lesson.
- Create a cross-curricular extension by discussing the question: Do you think that this is similar to the process the Founding Fathers used when they crafted the Constitution of the United States of America?

Assigning Value Concluding Activities

- Distribute the Assigning Value Exit Ticket (Appendix A). Ask students to reflect on their learning about the skill of Assigning Value, and how orders of importance might be different depending on the situation we are faced with. Allow time for students to complete the exit ticket. Use this as a formative assessment to gain a better understanding of your students' readiness to effectively practice the skill.
- If desired, complete the Group Using Assigning Value (Appendix A) to track students' progress with the skill.
- If desired, use the Evaluative Thinking Student Observation Rubric (Appendix A) to assess and quantify individual students' mastery.
- Ask students to retrieve their Evaluative Thinking Avatar (Handout I.4). In the Assigning Value box, they should either record the main ideas about the thinking skill or illustrate their avatar using the skill of Assigning Value.

Bibliography

Lionni, L. (1960). *Inch by inch*. New York: I. Obolensky.

Mosel, A. (1968). *Tikki tikki tembo*. New York: Holt, Rinehart and Winston.

Wise Brown, M. (1999) *The important book*. New York: HarperCollins Publishers.

CHAPTER 4

Sub-Skill 4

Discussing Gray Area

TABLE 4.1
Assigning Value Sub-Skill Outline

	Thinking Skill Outline
Focus Questions	❏ What happens when a question doesn't have just one right answer? ❏ Are values always clear-cut?
Lesson 1	*Opposing Values* ❏ **Trade Book Focus:** *The Wisdom Bird: A Tale of Solomon and Sheba* by Sheldon Oberman ❏ **Practice Activity:** *The Frog Prince*: Seeing Both Sides
Lesson 2	*Exceptions to Rules* ❏ **Fairytale Focus:** *Puss in Boots* by Charles Perrault ❏ **Practice Activity:** Fairytale Ethics: Students read a variety of fairytales to analyze the proverb "Honesty is the best policy."
Authentic Application Activity	*Socratic Seminar* ❏ **Trade Book Focus:** *We Found a Hat* by Jon Klassen ❏ **Socratic Seminar:** Discussing gray areas based on readings from fairytales.

EVALUATIVE THINKING for Advanced Learners, Grades 3–5

Discussing Gray Area Lesson 1: Opposing Values

Objective: Understand that some ideas, like values, leave room for interpretation and debate. We call this "wiggle room" *gray area*.

Materials

- Handout 4.1: Discussing Gray Area Anchor Chart (one for display)
- *The Wisdom Bird: A Tale of Solomon and Sheba* by Sheldon Oberman (teacher's copy)
- Handout 4.2: Read Aloud Reflection (one per student)
- Handout 4.3: *The Frog Prince* Story (one per student)
- Handout 4.4: What's Your Reason? (one per student)
- Handout 4.5: Seeing Both Sides—The King's View (duplicated as needed)
- Handout 4.6: Seeing Both Sides—The Princess' View (duplicated as needed)

Whole Group Introduction

- Introduce the following scenario to the group:
  - Every day, you ride the bus home from school. Today, your mom told you that after school you need to go run an errand with her, so you know you should be ready to go as soon as you get home. At recess, your best friend invites you to ride the bus home with them to play a new game they've just gotten. They tell you that their mom said that it would be ok. You really want to play the game, but you remember what your mom said that morning about having things to do after school. What do you do?
- Elicit some thoughts from students. Guide the discussion with some of the following:
  - What are the facts here? (You know your mom said to come home; your friend has asked you to come over; your friend says their mom agrees.)
  - What are your *interests/motivations*? (You don't really want to run errands, and you do want to play with your friend.)
  - What are your *values*? (You want to do what your mom asked [responsibility], but you also trust your friend and your friend's mom [loyalty, trust, your own self-interest].)

- What *rules* do you need to follow? (Do what your mom said or do what you want?)
❏ Using this discussion, lead students to understand that this is a question that leaves some room for doubt. There isn't necessarily a super clear answer here. Values, rules, and interests can pull in different directions.
❏ Tell students that when we don't have a clear answer and can see both sides of a situation, we can call that "gray area." This means there is not a simple, black-and-white (clear) answer. We must recognize as many aspects of a problem as we can in order to discuss the gray area and determine what the right solution is for ourselves. Share the Gray Area Anchor Chart (Handout 4.1).

Read Aloud Activity

❏ Introduce the story to the students. Tell them that in this story, King Solomon makes a promise to his friend, Queen Sheba. Both Sheba and Solomon are regarded as being very wise, but this promise puts them in a tricky situation.
❏ Read the story aloud. Pause to think aloud at various intervals, pointing out the *facts*, *interests*, *values*, and *rules* you notice in both Solomon and Sheba.
❏ Guide students in completing the Read Aloud Reflection page (Handout 4.2) to visually lay out the gray area conflict presented in the book: Should Solomon keep his promise or break it to save the birds' colors? Key understandings are outlined in Box 4.1.
❏ Discuss: How do the characters' values affect their behavior?

Box 4.1: *The Wisdom Bird: A Tale of Solomon and Sheba* Key Understandings

❏ *Story conflict summary*: Solomon must decide whether to keep his promise to Queen Sheba and cause all birds in the world to lose their beaks or break his promise and go back on his word.
❏ *Facts*: Both Solomon and Sheba agree that they are both very wise. They both agree that birds are important.
❏ *Values*: Solomon values the creatures of the world, as well as showing integrity by keeping his promises. Sheba values learning and wisdom.

Handout 4.1: Discussing Gray Area Anchor Chart

DISCUSSING GRAY AREA

DEBATING QUESTIONS WITH NO SINGLE CORRECT ANSWER

Handout 4.2: Read Aloud Reflection
The Wisdom Bird: A Tale of Solomon and Sheba by Sheldon Oberman

Name: _____

Describe the main conflict in the story:

FACTS:
What facts do Solomon and Sheba disagree on?

Agree on?

VALUES:
How do Solomon and Sheba's values differ?

How are they alike?

INTERESTS:
How do Solomon and Sheba's interests/motivations differ?

How are they alike?

POLICIES/RULES:
How do the rules Solomon and Sheba live by differ?

How are they similar?

DISCUSS: How do the characters' values affect their behavior? Do they ever have to choose between values? How do they choose?

EVALUATIVE THINKING for Advanced Learners, Grades 3–5

> ❏ *Interests*: Solomon and Sheba both seek to learn; they both want to understand things and grow in wisdom.
> ❏ *Policies/rules*: Both Solomon and Sheba were willing to re-think their original promises/deals in order to do what was right. They valued keeping their word, but were willing to bend this rule to act with wisdom and care.

Skill Development Activity

❏ For this activity, you'll be repeating the read-aloud activity with a new story. Distribute *The Frog Prince* story (Handout 4.3). Ask students to read and respond to the "consider and connect" questions in pairs or small groups. Questions are outlined in Table 4.2.

❏ As a whole group, discuss major takeaways. Distribute the What's Your Reason? thinking page (Handout 4.4) to help students organize their thoughts, discussing reasoning as a whole group and taking time to note varying or alternate viewpoints raised. Draw from the connect and consider sections in the story to support reasoning. Examples of this might include:

- *Facts*: The princess and the king disagree on the nature of the promise made, and if the promise should be upheld.
- *Values*: The king values integrity, while the princess values her own comfort. It seems they both value how others view them.
- *Interests*: The king has no interest in the matter with the frog, other than ensuring that his daughter acts with integrity. The princess is interested in maintaining her own comfort.
- *Policies/rules*: The king has a personal policy that a promise made should be a promise kept. The princess does not seem to care for this rule.

❏ Divide students into teams of three or four students. Distribute *one* perspective page (Handout 4.5, Handout 4.6) to each team. Teams will take on the perspective of either the king or the princess from the story. They will consider the perspective, choices, and values of that character to take a stand on how their values and choices align. Students should be able to draw on responses to the connect and consider questions from the story as well as responses recorded on Handout 4.4 to frame the thinking of each character.

❏ Give students some time to work on analyzing their character's viewpoint within the story *The Frog Prince*. Circulate, asking students to

Handout 4.3: Evaluating Values
The Frog Prince

 **CONSIDER**: what does the text say?

 **CONNECT**: How does that connect to the focus skill?

Name: _____

In olden times, when wishing still did some good, there lived a king whose daughters were all beautiful, but the youngest was so beautiful that the sun itself, who, indeed, has seen so much, marveled every time it shone upon her face. In the vicinity of the king's castle there was a large, dark forest, and in this forest, beneath an old linden tree, there was a well. In the heat of the day the princess would go out into the forest and sit on the edge of the cool well. To pass the time she would take a golden ball, throw it into the air, and then catch it. It was her favorite plaything.

Now one day it happened that the princess's golden ball did not fall into her hands, that she held up high, but instead it fell to the ground and rolled right into the water. The princess followed it with her eyes, but the ball disappeared, and the well was so deep that she could not see its bottom. Then she began to cry. She cried louder and louder, and she could not console herself.

As she was thus lamenting, someone called out to her, "What is the matter with you, princess? Your crying would turn a stone to pity."

She looked around to see where the voice was coming from and saw a frog, who had stuck his thick, ugly head out of the water. "Oh, it's you, old water-splasher," she said. "I am crying because my golden ball has fallen into the well."

"Be still and stop crying," answered the frog. I can help you, but what will you give me if I bring back your plaything?"

"Whatever you want, dear frog," she said, "my clothes, my pearls and precious stones, and even the golden crown that I am wearing."

The frog answered, "I do not want your clothes, your pearls and precious stones, nor your golden crown, but if you will love me and accept me as a companion and playmate, and let me sit next to you at your table and eat from your golden plate and drink from your cup and sleep in your bed, if you will promise this to me, then I'll dive down and bring your golden ball back to you."

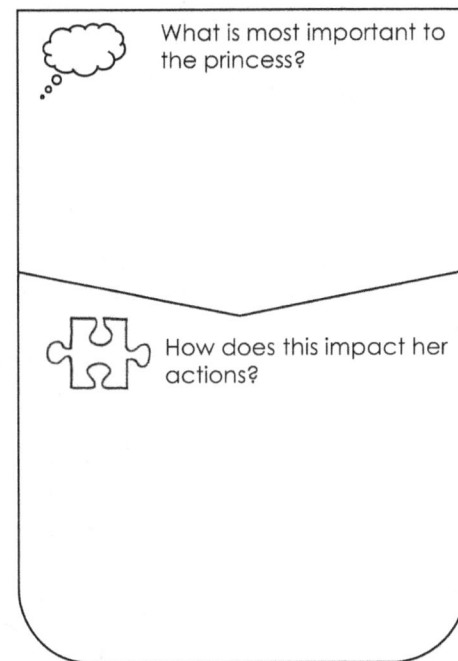

What is most important to the princess?

How does this impact her actions?

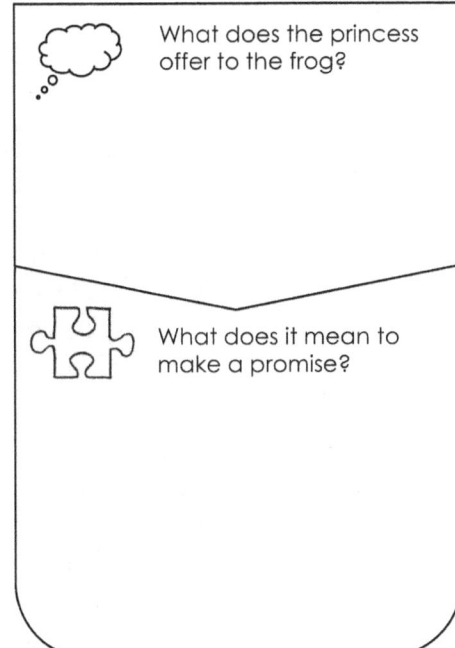

What does the princess offer to the frog?

What does it mean to make a promise?

Handout 4.3: Evaluating Values
The Frog Prince

Name: _____

 **CONSIDER**: what does the text say?

 **CONNECT**: How does that connect to the focus skill?

"Oh, yes," she said, "I promise all of that to you if you will just bring the ball back to me." But she thought, "What is this stupid frog trying to say? He just sits here in the water with his own kind and croaks. He cannot be a companion to a human."

As soon as the frog heard her say "yes" he stuck his head under and dove to the bottom. He paddled back up a short time later with the golden ball in his mouth and threw it onto the grass. The princess was filled with joy when she saw her beautiful plaything once again, picked it up, and ran off.

"Wait, wait," called the frog, "take me along. I cannot run as fast as you." But what did it help him, that he croaked out after her as loudly as he could? She paid no attention to him, but instead hurried home and soon forgot the poor frog, who had to return again to his well.

The next day the princess was sitting at the table with the king and all the people of the court, and was eating from her golden plate when something came creeping up the marble steps: plip, plop, plip, plop. As soon as it reached the top, there came a knock at the door, and a voice called out, "Princess, youngest, open the door for me!"

She ran to see who was outside. She opened the door, and the frog was sitting there. Frightened, she slammed the door shut and returned to the table. The king saw that her heart was pounding and asked, "My child, why are you afraid? Is there a giant outside the door who wants to get you?"

"Oh, no," she answered. "it is a disgusting frog."

"What does the frog want from you?"

"Oh, father dear, yesterday when I was sitting near the well in the forest and playing, my golden ball fell into the water. And because I was crying so much, the frog brought it back, and because he insisted, I promised him that he could be my companion, but I didn't think that he could leave his water. But now he is just outside the door and wants to come in."

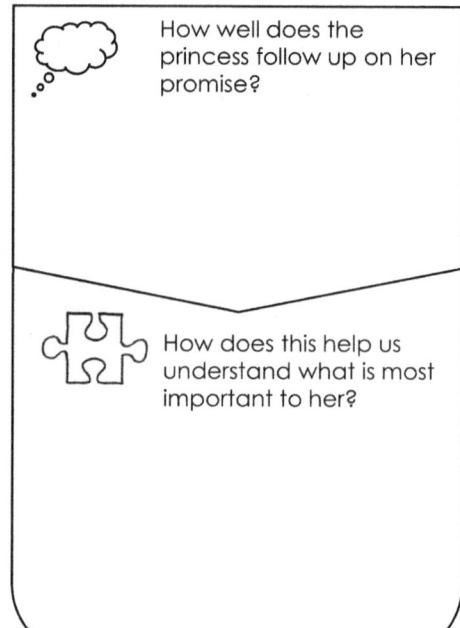

How well does the princess follow up on her promise?

How does this help us understand what is most important to her?

Describe how the princess treats the frog.

Does the princess value promises (keeping her word)?

Handout 4.3: Evaluating Values
The Frog Prince

Name: _____

CONSIDER: what does the text say?

CONNECT: How does that connect to the focus skill?

Just then there came a second knock at the door, and a voice called out:

> Youngest daughter of the king,
> Open up the door for me,
> Don't you know what yesterday,
> You said to me down by the well?
> Youngest daughter of the king,
> Open up the door for me.

The king said, "What you have promised, you must keep. Go and let the frog in."

She went and opened the door, and the frog hopped in, then followed her up to her chair. He sat there and called out, "Lift me up next to you."

She hesitated, until finally the king commanded her to do it. When the frog was seated next to her he said, "Now push your golden plate closer, so we can eat together."

She did it, but one could see that she did not want to. The frog enjoyed his meal, but for her every bite stuck in her throat. Finally he said, "I have eaten all I want and am tired. Now carry me to your room and make your bed so that we can go to sleep."

The princess began to cry and was afraid of the cold frog and did not dare to even touch him, and yet he was supposed to sleep in her beautiful, clean bed.

The king became angry and said, "You should not despise someone who has helped you in time of need."

She picked him up with two fingers, carried him upstairs, and set him in a corner. As she was lying in bed, he came creeping up to her and said, "I am tired, and I want to sleep as well as you do. Pick me up or I'll tell your father."

With that she became bitterly angry and threw him against the wall with all her might. "Now you will have your peace, you disgusting frog!"

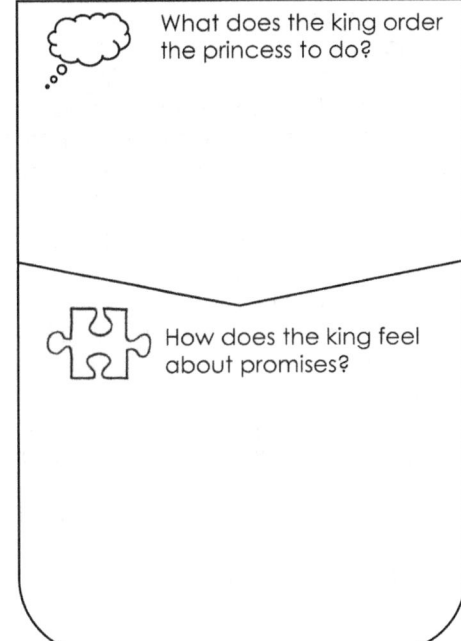

What does the king order the princess to do?

How does the king feel about promises?

How does the frog get the princess to put him in the bed?

What does this tell you about the princess?

Handout 4.3: Evaluating Values
The Frog Prince

Name: _____

 CONSIDER: what does the text say?

 **CONNECT:** How does that connect to the focus skill?

But when he fell down, he was not a frog, but a prince with beautiful friendly eyes. And he was now, according to her father's will, her dear companion and husband. He told her how he had been enchanted by a wicked witch, and that she alone could have rescued him from the well, and that tomorrow they would go together to his kingdom. Then they fell asleep.

The next morning, just as the sun was waking them, a carriage pulled up, drawn by eight horses. They had white ostrich feathers on their heads and were outfitted with chains of gold. At the rear stood the young king's servant, faithful Heinrich. Faithful Heinrich had been so saddened by his master's transformation into a frog that he had had to place three iron bands around his heart to keep it from bursting in grief and sorrow. The carriage was to take the king back to his kingdom. Faithful Heinrich lifted them both inside and took his place at the rear. He was filled with joy over the redemption. After they had gone a short distance, the prince heard a crack from behind, as though something had broken.

He turned around and said, "Heinrich, the carriage is breaking apart."

 What happens when the princess throws the frog down?

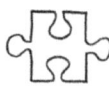 The story doesn't tell us, but how do you think the princess responded?

> No, my lord, the carriage it's not,
> But one of the bands surrounding my heart,
> That suffered such great pain,
> When you were sitting in the well,
> When you were a frog.

Once again, and then once again the prince heard a cracking sound and thought that the carriage was breaking apart, but it was the bands springing from faithful Heinrich's heart because his master was now redeemed and happy.

 Describe Heinrich's reaction to the prince.

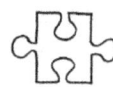 What does this tell you about the prince? What about Heinrich?

Handout 4.4: What's Your Reason?

Name: _____

Describe the main conflict in the story:

FACTS: What facts do the princess and the king disagree on? Agree on?	**VALUES:** How do the princess and the king's values differ? How are they alike?
INTERESTS: How do the princess and the king's interests/motivations differ? How are they alike?	**POLICIES/RULES:** How do the rules the princess and the king live by differ? How are they similar?

DISCUSS: How do the values of the king and the princess affect their behavior? Whose values are closest to your own?

Handout 4.5: Seeing Both Sides-The King's View

Name: _____

What facts does the king know about the problem?

What rules or policies of behavior does the king live by?

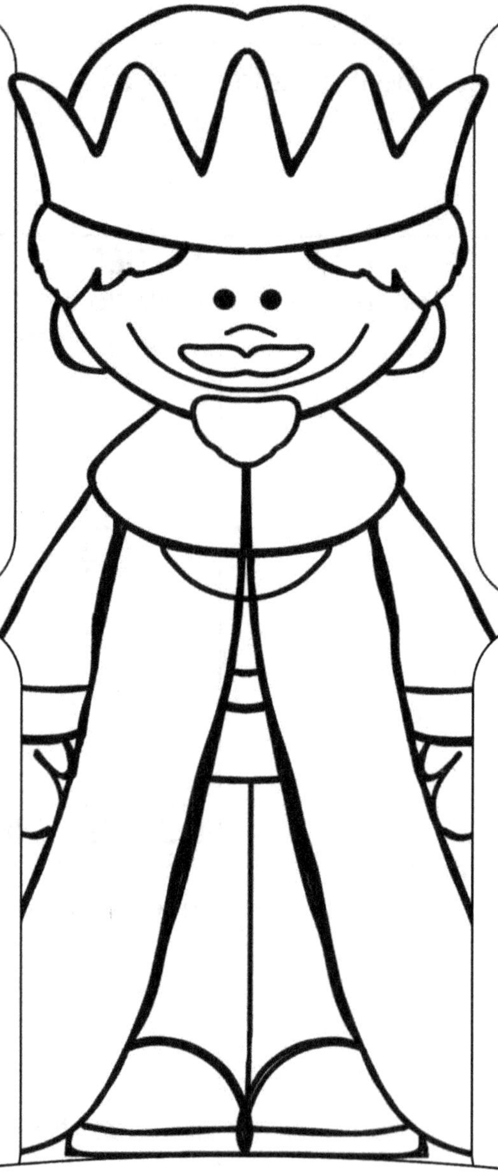

How would you describe the character of the king?

What does the king feel is the best course of action? Why?

What is the king's CORE VALUE? (Think: what value(s) are most important to him?)

EXTEND: Create a script of a speech that the king could give to the princess to share his perspective with her. How will you share your core values?

Handout 4.6: Seeing Both Sides-The Princess' View

Name: _____

What facts does the princess know about the problem?

What rules or policies of behavior does the princess live by?

How would you describe the character of the princess?

What does the princess feel is the best course of action? Why?

What is the princess' CORE VALUE? (Think: what value(s) are most important to him?)

EXTEND: Create a script of a speech that the princess could give to the king to share her perspective with him. How will you share your core values?

really dig into the values and motivations that were important to their character. Help students to dig into the ambiguity:
- Should the king force his daughter to keep a promise if it will make her completely miserable? Is it really important to value a promise over one's happiness?
- Should the princess go back on her word just because it would make her uncomfortable? Is your temporary comfort worth more than the value of keeping your word?

- As groups finish, ask them to look at the "Extend" activity. Teams should work collaboratively to come up with a short speech that the princess/king could present to the other character. Their speech should explain their viewpoint and values and defend their actions.
- Ask a few groups to share their speeches. Who was most convincing? Why?
- As a whole group, discuss the following: Who was right? Who was wrong? Where is the gray area?
- As an optional extension, invite students to write and present a speech from the perspective of their chosen character, defending their own point of view.

Discussing Gray Area Lesson 2: Exceptions to Rules

Objective: Discuss gray area in values and exceptions to rules in the context of familiar stories.

Materials

- Handout 4.7: *Puss in Boots* by Charles Perrault (one per student or teacher's copy)
- Handout 4.8: Read Aloud Reflection Page (one per student)
- Handout 4.9a: Prior to Reading Concept Builder (one per student)
- Handout 4.9b: After Reading Concept Analysis (one per student)
- Handout 4.10: *The Emperor's New Clothes* Story (duplicated as needed)
- Handout 4.11: *Rumpelstiltskin* Story (duplicated as needed)
- Handout 4.12: *Hansel and Gretel* Story (duplicated as needed)

Whole Group Introduction

❑ Remind students that gray area happens when an answer to a question is unclear. Tell them that gray area also describes places where rules might have exceptions. Pose the following question: Are there exceptions to rules? Let's think about this...
  - We always go to recess outside. *Except...*
  - We never eat dessert for breakfast. *Except...*
  - Always raise your hand before speaking in our classroom. *Except...*
  - Never tell a lie. *Except...*

❑ This is gray area! We know rules are great for keeping us safe, healthy, and organized. But if we are going to be fair and consider all perspectives, we must know that there is bound to be gray area that arises from

TABLE 4.2
The Frog Prince Connect and Consider Outline

Story Page	Consider		Connect
Page 1	The princess' ball is what is most important to her.	→	Because of this, she is willing to make a deal with the frog to get it back.
	The princess offers the frog whatever he wants: her jewels, her crown, her clothes, etc.	→	When you make a promise, you are ensuring someone else that you will do what you say.
Page 2	The princess does not follow through at all with her promise.	→	We can see that she cares mostly about herself and her own comfort.
	The princess is cruel, and makes the frog feel unwelcome and scorned.	→	The princess values her own comfort over keeping her promises.
Page 3	The king orders the princess to keep her promise to the frog.	→	The king feels that it's important to keep one's word. He values integrity.
	The frog threatens to tell the princess' father if she does not put him in the bed.	→	The princess values her father's opinion more than she values the frog.
Page 4	The frog turns into a prince when the princess throws him down.	→	The princess was likely shocked and amazed. Perhaps she felt embarrassed.
	Heinrich feels overcome with joy, so much so that his heart is bursting with happiness.	→	The prince is clearly someone that inspires love and loyalty. Heinrich values faithfulness and loyalty.

time to time. It's very hard to make always/never statements, as there can be exceptions from time to time.

Read Aloud Activity

- ❑ Distribute the story *Puss in Boots* (Handout 4.7) to each student. You may also choose to read it aloud with the pages displayed for student view. Read it aloud, pausing to discuss the "consider and connect" questions on each page. Pay special attention to how the cat's dishonesty may or may not be justified.
- ❑ After you read, distribute and ask students to complete the Read Aloud Reflection page (Handout 4.8) in pairs. Circulate, helping students refer back to the story text for clues to support their answers. See Box 4.2 for key understandings to target.

Box 4.2: *Puss in Boots* Key Understandings

- ❑ *Story summary*: The youngest son of a miller inherits only a cat when his father dies. The cat uses trickery, telling small white lies and allowing others to assume things about him, to gain the boy wealth and status.
- ❑ *Positive traits exhibited*: The cat is loyal to his master and demonstrates initiative in improving his own situation.
- ❑ *Negative traits exhibited*: Puss lies to get into his advanced position. The boy agrees to the con. Others exhibit greed and/or selfishness.
- ❑ *Values*:
  - The cat values comfort. All of his actions have a goal of making his and his master's lives more comfortable.
  - The Marquis values the cat; he follows each direction given to him by the animal, allowing lies to be told on his behalf and following suit in upholding those lies.
  - The king values the adoration of others and seeks for others to view him as wealthy and powerful.
  - The princess values the charm and handsomeness of the Marquis.
- ❑ *Sample moral*: Hard work and careful planning pay off. The cat worked hard to play his cunning tricks and this results in him living an easy life in a castle.

Handout 4.7: Exceptions
Puss in Boots by Charles Perrault

Name: _____

CONSIDER: what does the text say?

CONNECT: How does that connect to the focus skill?

There was a miller whose only inheritance to his three sons was his mill, his donkey, and his cat. The division was soon made. They hired neither a clerk nor an attorney, for they would have eaten up all the poor patrimony. The eldest took the mill, the second the donkey, and the youngest nothing but the cat.

The poor young fellow was quite comfortless for having received so little. "My brothers," said he, "may make a handsome living by joining their shares together; but, for my part, after I have eaten up my cat, and made myself a muff from his skin, I must then die of hunger."

The cat, who heard all this, but pretended otherwise, said to him with a grave and serious air, "Do not be so concerned, my good master. If you will but give me a bag, and have a pair of boots made for me, that I may scamper through the dirt and the brambles, then you shall see that you are not so poorly off with me as you imagine."

The cat's master did not build very much upon what he said. However, he had often seen him play a great many cunning tricks to catch rats and mice, such as hanging by his heels, or hiding himself in the meal, and pretending to be dead; so he did take some hope that he might give him some help in his miserable condition.

After receiving what he had asked for, the cat gallantly pulled on the boots and slung the bag about his neck. Holding its drawstrings in his forepaws, he went to a place where there was a great abundance of rabbits. He put some bran and greens into his bag, then stretched himself out as if he were dead. He thus waited for some young rabbits, not yet acquainted with the deceits of the world, to come and look into his bag.

He had scarcely lain down before he had what he wanted. A rash and foolish young rabbit jumped into his bag, and the master cat, immediately closed the strings, then took and killed him without pity.

Proud of his prey, he went with it to the palace, and asked to speak with his majesty. He was shown upstairs into the king's apartment, and, making a low bow, said to him, "Sir, I have brought you a rabbit from my noble lord, the Master of Carabas" (for that was the title which the cat was pleased to give his master).

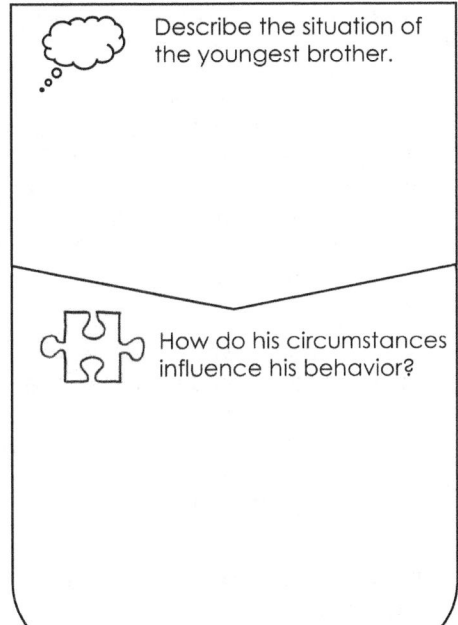

Describe the situation of the youngest brother.

How do his circumstances influence his behavior?

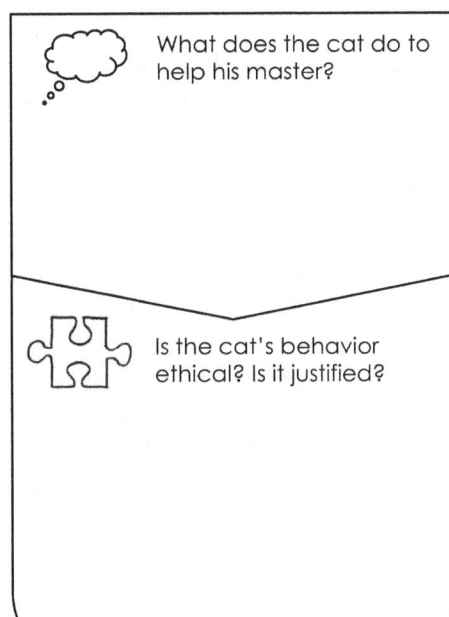

What does the cat do to help his master?

Is the cat's behavior ethical? Is it justified?

Handout 4.7: Exceptions
Puss in Boots by Charles Perrault

Name: _____

"Tell your master," said the king, "that I thank him, and that I am very pleased with his gift."

Another time he went and hid himself in a grain field. He again held his bag open, and when a brace of partridges ran into it, he drew the strings, and caught them both. He presented these to the king, as he had done before with the rabbit. The king, in like manner, received the partridges with great pleasure, and gave him a tip. The cat continued, from time to time for two or three months, to take game to his majesty from his master.

One day, when he knew for certain that the king would be taking a drive along the riverside with his daughter, the most beautiful princess in the world, he said to his master, "If you will follow my advice your fortune is made. All you must do is to go and bathe yourself in the river at the place I show you, then leave the rest to me."

The Marquis of Carabas did what the cat advised him to, without knowing why. While he was bathing the king passed by, and the cat began to cry out, "Help! Help! My Lord Marquis of Carabas is going to be drowned."

At this noise the king put his head out of the coach window, and, finding it was the cat who had so often brought him such good game, he commanded his guards to run immediately to the assistance of his lordship the Marquis of Carabas. While they were drawing the poor Marquis out of the river, the cat came up to the coach and told the king that, while his master was bathing, some rogues had come by and stolen his clothes, even though he had cried out, "Thieves! Thieves!" several times, as loud as he could. In truth, the cunning cat had hidden the clothes under a large stone.

The king immediately commanded the officers of his wardrobe to run and fetch one of his best suits for the Lord Marquis of Carabas.

The king received him very courteously. And, because the king's fine clothes gave him a striking appearance (for he was very handsome and well proportioned), the king's daughter took a secret inclination to him. The Marquis of Carabas had only to cast two or three respectful and somewhat tender glances at her but she fell head over heels in love with him. The king asked him to enter the coach and join them on their drive.

2

 CONSIDER: what does the text say?

 **CONNECT**: How does that connect to the focus skill?

 The cat's deception has worked on the king. Who else is he fooling?

 Why must the cat lie to both the king and his master?

 How has the cat has prepared for this situation?

 What does the complexity of the cat's tricks tell you about the cat's character?

Handout 4.7: Exceptions
Puss in Boots by Charles Perrault

 CONSIDER: what does the text say?

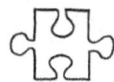 **CONNECT**: How does that connect to the focus skill?

Name: _____

The cat, quite overjoyed to see how his project was succeeding, ran on ahead. Meeting some countrymen who were mowing a meadow, he said to them, "My good fellows, if you do not tell the king that the meadow you are mowing belongs to my Lord Marquis of Carabas, you shall be chopped up like mincemeat."

The king did not fail to ask the mowers whose meadow it was that they were mowing.

"It belongs to my Lord Marquis of Carabas," they answered altogether, for the cat's threats had frightened them.

"You see, sir," said the Marquis, "this is a meadow which never fails to yield a plentiful harvest every year."

The master cat, still running on ahead, met with some reapers, and said to them, "My good fellows, if you do not tell the king that all this grain belongs to the Marquis of Carabas, you shall be chopped up like mincemeat."

The king, who passed by a moment later, asked them whose grain it was that they were reaping.

"It belongs to my Lord Marquis of Carabas," replied the reapers, which pleased both the king and the marquis. The king congratulated him for his fine harvest. The master cat continued to run ahead and said the same words to all he met. The king was astonished at the vast estates of the Lord Marquis of Carabas.

The master cat came at last to a stately castle, the lord of which was an ogre, the richest that had ever been known. All the lands which the king had just passed by belonged to this castle. The cat, who had taken care to inform himself who this ogre was and what he could do, asked to speak with him, saying he could not pass so near his castle without having the honor of paying his respects to him.

The ogre received him as civilly as an ogre could do, and invited him to sit down. "I have heard," said the cat, "that you are able to change yourself into any kind of creature that you have a mind to. You can, for example, transform yourself into a lion, an elephant, or the like."

"That is true," answered the ogre very briskly; "and to convince you, I shall now become a lion."

How is the cat convincing others to lie?

Why doesn't anybody tell on the cat?

Describe the actions of the marquis.

Is he being truthful? What can we say about his values?

3

Handout 4.7: Exceptions
Puss in Boots by Charles Perrault

Name: _____

CONSIDER: what does the text say?

CONNECT: How does that connect to the focus skill?

The cat was so terrified at the sight of a lion so near him that he leaped onto the roof, which caused him even more difficulty, because his boots were of no use at all to him in walking on the tiles. However, the ogre resumed his natural form, and the cat came down, saying that he had been very frightened indeed.

"I have further been told," said the cat, "that you can also transform yourself into the smallest of animals, for example, a rat or a mouse. But I can scarcely believe that. I must admit to you that I think that that would be quite impossible."

"Impossible!" cried the ogre. "You shall see!"

He immediately changed himself into a mouse and began to run about the floor. As soon as the cat saw this, he fell upon him and ate him up.

Meanwhile the king, who saw this fine castle of the ogre's as he passed, decided to go inside. The cat, who heard the noise of his majesty's coach running over the drawbridge, ran out and said to the king, "Your majesty is welcome to this castle of my Lord Marquis of Carabas."

"What! my Lord Marquis," cried the king, "and does this castle also belong to you? There can be nothing finer than this court and all the stately buildings which surround it. Let us go inside, if you don't mind."

The marquis gave his hand to the princess, and followed the king, who went first. They passed into a spacious hall, where they found a magnificent feast, which the ogre had prepared for his friends, who were coming to visit him that very day, but dared not to enter, knowing the king was there.

His majesty was perfectly charmed with the good qualities of my Lord Marquis of Carabas, as was his daughter, who had fallen violently in love with him, and, seeing the vast estate he possessed, said to him, after having drunk five or six glasses, "It will be your own fault, my Lord Marquis, if you do not become my son-in-law."

The marquis, making several low bows, accepted the honor which his majesty conferred upon him, and forthwith, that very same day, married the princess.

The cat became a great lord, and never again ran after mice, except for entertainment.

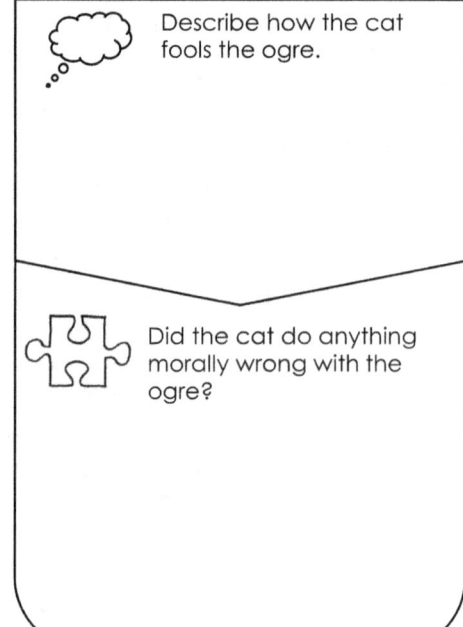

Describe how the cat fools the ogre.

Did the cat do anything morally wrong with the ogre?

Describe how the princess falls in love with the marquis.

Based on how she decided she loved him, what can we say about the princess' values?

Handout 4.8: Read Aloud Reflection
Puss in Boots by Charles Perrault

Name: _____

Describe POSITIVE values characters demonstrated in the story.	Describe NEGATIVE values characters demonstrated in the story.

People value different things, such as education, loyalty, honesty, security (money), appearances, power, or happiness. Think about what the characters in this story value most. Describe in the table below.

The CAT values…	I know because…
The MARQUIS values…	I know because…
The KING values…	I know because…
The PRINCESS values…	I know because…

Write a moral for this story that gives readers a lesson on a specific value that they could learn from reading.

❏ *Discuss the following*: Where was the gray area? How can we tell what each character values by the morals/values they were willing to bend/break?

Skill Development Activity

❏ Tell students that today's activity will involve reading a familiar fairytale and thinking about the gray area surrounding one key value: honesty. Students will be divided into teams, each working on a different tale, to discover what they can about the concept of honesty as it relates to a different situation and set of characters.
❏ Remind teams that as we read, we will be looking at how each story focuses on the gray area regarding a single moral: honesty. Ask students to think about their own feelings about honesty using the graphic organizer provided on the pre-reading worksheet (Handout 4.9a). Discuss this graphic organizer as a whole group. Ensure that all students have a strong understanding of the concept of honesty.
  ■ *Teacher's note*: You may want to duplicate Handout 4.9a and 4.9b front-to-back on a single sheet, or you may choose to duplicate these pages separately. Either way, these two graphic organizers will be consistent for all groups, regardless of which fairytale they work with.
❏ Divide the group into three teams and distribute one of the provided fairytale booklets to each group. The three included fairytales are *The Emperor's New Clothes* (Handout 4.10), *Rumpelstiltskin* (Handout 4.11), and *Hansel and Gretel* (Handout 4.12).
  ■ *Teacher's note*: The three provided fairytales are scaffolded in terms of both text complexity and abstraction related to the concept of honesty. *The Emperor's New Clothes* is intended to be the simplest text, *Rumpelstiltskin* of moderate difficulty, and *Hansel and Gretel* the most complex.
❏ Allow some time for teams to work through their individual fairytales, answering the questions that arise throughout the story in the "consider and connect" panels.
❏ Circulate, helping clarify and connect students' thinking. Ensure students are pausing to answer the questions that are posed as they read, rather than waiting until the end of the story to complete them. See Table 4.4 (*The Emperor's New Clothes*), Table 4.5 (*Rumpelstiltskin*), and Table 4.6 (*Hansel and Gretel*) for outlines of these questions to guide your discussion with students.

Handout 4.9a: Prior to Reading-Concept Builder

Name: _____

Definition	Characteristics/Actions
HONESTY	
Examples	Non-Examples

Why do people value honesty?

How true is the proverb, "Honesty is the best policy"? Explain.

Handout 4.9b: After Reading-Concept Analysis

Name: _____

List times in the story when characters demonstrated dishonesty.

Of your examples above, which would you say are justified? Think about why you feel the way you do.

They say, "Honesty is the best policy". Rewrite this proverb based on the gray area you see regarding honesty after reading this story.

Handout 4.10: Gray Area Analysis
The Emperor's New Clothes by Hans Christian Andersen

 CONSIDER: what does the text say?

 CONNECT: How does that connect to the focus skill?

Name: _____

Many years ago there was an Emperor so exceedingly fond of new clothes that he spent all his money on being well dressed. He cared nothing about reviewing his soldiers, going to the theatre, or going for a ride in his carriage, except to show off his new clothes. He had a coat for every hour of the day, and instead of saying, as one might, about any other ruler, "The King's in council," here they always said. "The Emperor's in his dressing room."

> Starting here, highlight each time someone is **dishonest**.

In the great city where he lived, life was always gay. Every day many strangers came to town, and among them one day came two swindlers.

They let it be known they were weavers, and they said they could weave the most magnificent fabrics imaginable. Not only were their colors and patterns uncommonly fine, but clothes made of this cloth had a wonderful way of becoming invisible to anyone who was unfit for his office, or who was unusually stupid.

"Those would be just the clothes for me," thought the Emperor. "If I wore them I would be able to discover which men in my empire are unfit for their posts. And I could tell the wise men from the fools. Yes, I certainly must get some of the stuff woven for me right away." He paid the two swindlers a large sum of money to start work at once.

They set up two looms and pretended to weave, though there was nothing on the looms. All the finest silk and the purest old thread which they demanded went into their traveling bags, while they worked the empty looms far into the night.

"I'd like to know how those weavers are getting on with the cloth," the Emperor thought, but he felt slightly uncomfortable when he remembered that those who were unfit for their position would not be able to see the fabric. It couldn't have been that he doubted himself, yet he thought he'd rather send someone else to see how things were going. The whole town knew about the cloth's peculiar power, and all were impatient to find out how stupid their neighbors were.

 Give three adjectives to describe the swindlers, and three to describe the emperor.

What differences and/or similarities do you notice?

 How does the emperor view himself? How does he view others?

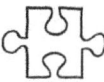 What things do you think the emperor values?

Handout 4.10: Gray Area Analysis
The Emperor's New Clothes by Hans Christian Andersen

Name: _____

"I'll send my honest old minister to the weavers," the Emperor decided. "He'll be the best one to tell me how the material looks, for he's a sensible man and no one does his duty better."

So the honest old minister went to the room where the two swindlers sat working away at their empty looms.

"Heaven help me," he thought as his eyes flew wide open, "I can't see anything at all". But he did not say so.

Both the swindlers begged him to be so kind as to come near to approve the excellent pattern, the beautiful colors. They pointed to the empty looms, and the poor old minister stared as hard as he dared. He couldn't see anything, because there was nothing to see. "Heaven have mercy," he thought. "Can it be that I'm a fool? I'd have never guessed it, and not a soul must know. Am I unfit to be the minister? It would never do to let on that I can't see the cloth."

"Don't hesitate to tell us what you think of it," said one of the weavers.

"Oh, it's beautiful - it's enchanting." The old minister peered through his spectacles. "Such a pattern, what colors! I'll be sure to tell the Emperor how delighted I am with it."

"We're pleased to hear that," the swindlers said. They proceeded to name all the colors and to explain the intricate pattern. The old minister paid the closest attention, so that he could tell it all to the Emperor. And so he did.

The swindlers at once asked for more money, more silk and gold thread, to get on with the weaving. But it all went into their pockets. Not a thread went into the looms, though they worked at their weaving as hard as ever.

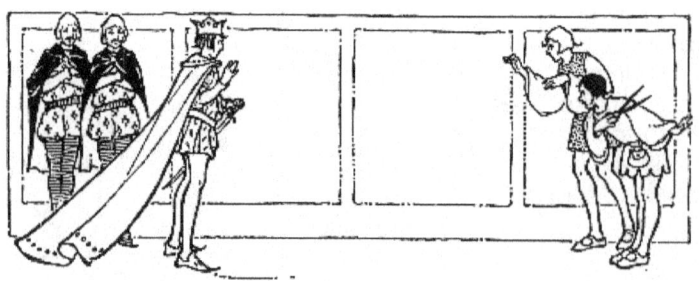

 CONSIDER: what does the text say?

 **CONNECT:** How does that connect to the focus skill?

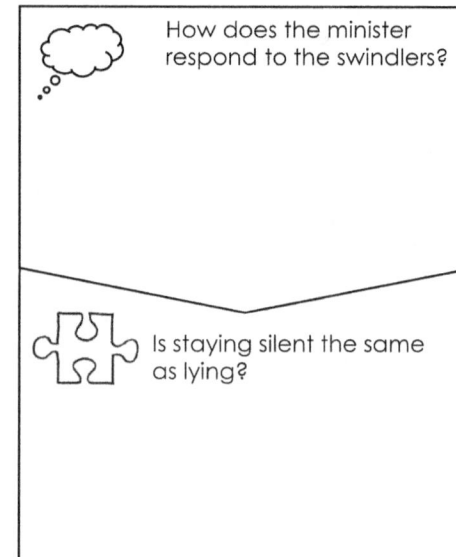

How does the minister respond to the swindlers?

Is staying silent the same as lying?

Why do you think the "honest" minister lies?

Is there something the minister values more than honesty?

Handout 4.10: Gray Area Analysis
The Emperor's New Clothes by Hans Christian Andersen

Name: _____

CONSIDER: what does the text say?

CONNECT: How does that connect to the focus skill?

The Emperor presently sent another trustworthy official to see how the work progressed and how soon it would be ready. The same thing happened to him that had happened to the minister. He looked and he looked, but as there was nothing to see in the looms he couldn't see anything.

"Isn't it a beautiful piece of goods?" the swindlers asked him, as they displayed and described their imaginary pattern.

"I know I'm not stupid," the man thought, "so it must be that I'm unworthy of my good office. That's strange. I mustn't let anyone find it out, though." So he praised the material he did not see. He declared he was delighted with the beautiful colors and the exquisite pattern. To the Emperor he said, "It held me spellbound."

All the town was talking of this splendid cloth, and the Emperor wanted to see it for himself while it was still in the looms. Attended by a band of chosen men, among whom were his two old trusted officials-the ones who had been to the weavers-he set out to see the two swindlers. He found them weaving with might and main, but without a thread in their looms.

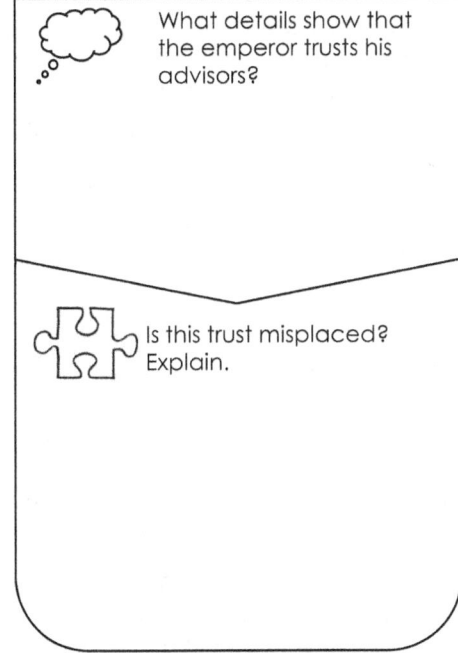

What details show that the emperor trusts his advisors?

Is this trust misplaced? Explain.

"Magnificent," said the two officials already duped. "Just look, Your Majesty, what colors! What a design!" They pointed to the empty looms, each supposing that the others could see the stuff.

"What's this?" thought the Emperor. "I can't see anything. This is terrible!

Am I a fool? Am I unfit to be the Emperor? What a thing to happen to me of all people! - Oh! It's very pretty," he said. "It has my highest approval." And he nodded approbation at the empty loom. Nothing could make him say that he couldn't see anything.

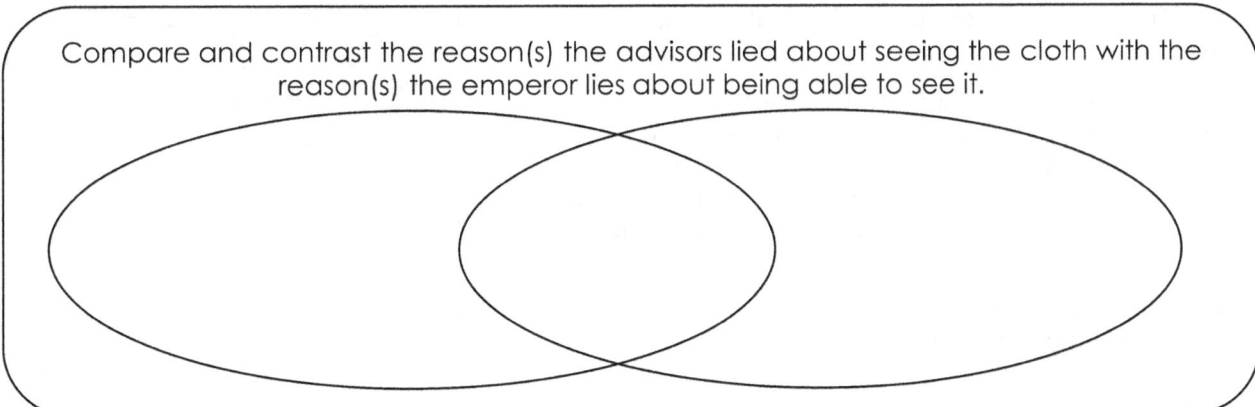

Compare and contrast the reason(s) the advisors lied about seeing the cloth with the reason(s) the emperor lies about being able to see it.

Handout 4.10: Gray Area Analysis
The Emperor's New Clothes by Hans Christian Andersen

Name: _____

 **CONSIDER:** what does the text say?

 **CONNECT:** How does that connect to the focus skill?

His whole retinue stared and stared. One saw no more than another, but they all joined the Emperor in exclaiming, "Oh! It's *very* pretty," and they advised him to wear clothes made of this wonderful cloth especially for the great procession he was soon to lead. "Magnificent! Excellent! Unsurpassed!" were bandied from mouth to mouth, and everyone did his best to seem well pleased. The Emperor gave each of the swindlers a cross to wear in his buttonhole, and the title of "Sir Weaver."

Before the procession the swindlers sat up all night and burned more than six candles, to show how busy they were finishing the Emperor's new clothes. They pretended to take the cloth off the loom. They made cuts in the air with huge scissors. And at last they said, "Now the Emperor's new clothes are ready for him."

Then the Emperor himself came with his noblest noblemen, and the swindlers each raised an arm as if they were holding something. They said, "These are the trousers, here's the coat, and this is the mantle," naming each garment. "All of them are as light as a spider web. One would almost think he had nothing on, but that's what makes them so fine."

"Exactly," all the noblemen agreed, though they could see nothing, for there was nothing to see.

"If Your Imperial Majesty will condescend to take your clothes off," said the swindlers, "we will help you on with your new ones here in front of the long mirror."

The Emperor undressed, and the swindlers pretended to put his new clothes on him, one garment after another. They took him around the waist and seemed to be fastening something - that was his train-as the Emperor turned round and round before the looking glass.

"How well Your Majesty's new clothes look. Aren't they becoming!" He heard on all sides, "That pattern, so perfect! Those colors, so suitable! It is a magnificent outfit."

 How do all the noblemen react to the "clothes"?

 What does this say about their values as a group?

 Is anyone truthful on this page?

 Are the people lying to others or themselves?

Handout 4.10: Gray Area Analysis
The Emperor's New Clothes by Hans Christian Andersen

Name: _____

 CONSIDER: what does the text say?

 **CONNECT**: How does that connect to the focus skill?

Then the minister of public processions announced: "Your Majesty's canopy is waiting outside."

"Well, I'm supposed to be ready," the Emperor said, and turned again for one last look in the mirror. "It is a remarkable fit, isn't it?" He seemed to regard his costume with the greatest interest.

The noblemen who were to carry his train stooped low and reached for the floor as if they were picking up his mantle. Then they pretended to lift and hold it high. They didn't dare admit they had nothing to hold.

So off went the Emperor in procession under his splendid canopy. Everyone in the streets and the windows said, "Oh, how fine are the Emperor's new clothes! Don't they fit him to perfection? And see his long train!" Nobody would confess that he couldn't see anything, for that would prove him either unfit for his position, or a fool. No costume the Emperor had worn before was ever such a complete success.

"But he hasn't got anything on," a little child said.

"Did you ever hear such innocent prattle?" said its father. And one person whispered to another what the child had said, "He hasn't anything on. A child says he hasn't anything on."

"But he hasn't got anything on!" the whole town cried out at last.

The Emperor shivered, for he suspected they were right. But he thought, "This procession has got to go on." So he walked more proudly than ever, as his noblemen held high the train that wasn't there at all.

 Describe the emperor's actions as he prepares to step outside.

 Why do you think he feels confident in going out?

 Who calls out the emperor's lack of clothes?

 What is different about this character from all the others in the story so far?

Handout 4.10: The Emperor's New Clothes Reflection

Name: _____

Fill in the blanks to follow the chain of events in The Emperor's New Clothes. Think about the reasons for deceit.

> The swindlers lied to the emperor because...

> The advisors all lied to the emperor because...

> The emperor decided to go outside without any clothes because...

> The child told the truth because...

> Why are people dishonest? Is lying to yourself the same as lying to others?

Handout 4.11: Gray Area Analysis
Rumpelstiltskin by the Brothers Grimm

Name: _____

 CONSIDER: what does the text say?

 **CONNECT**: How does that connect to the focus skill?

By the side of a wood, in a country a long way off, ran a fine stream of water; and upon the stream there stood a mill. The miller's house was close by, and the miller, you must know, had a very beautiful daughter.

Starting here, highlight each time someone is dishonest.

She was, moreover, very shrewd and clever; and the miller was so proud of her, that he one day told the king of the land, who used to come and hunt in the wood, that his daughter could spin gold out of straw.

Now this king was very fond of money; and when he heard the miller's boast his greediness was raised, and he sent for the girl to be brought before him. Then he led her to a chamber in his palace where there was a great heap of straw, and gave her a spinning-wheel, and said, 'All this must be spun into gold before morning, as you love your life.' It was in vain that the poor maiden said that it was only a silly boast of her father, for that she could do no such thing as spin straw into gold: the chamber door was locked, and she was left alone.

 Describe the miller and his daughter.

 Why does the miller lie about his daughter to the king?

 Describe the situation the daughter finds herself in.

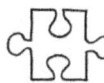 How did she get into this predicament?

Handout 4.11: Gray Area Analysis
Rumpelstiltskin by the Brothers Grimm

Name: _____

CONSIDER: what does the text say?

CONNECT: How does that connect to the focus skill?

She sat down in one corner of the room, and began to bewail her hard fate; when on a sudden the door opened, and a droll-looking little man hobbled in, and said, 'Good morrow to you, my good lass; what are you weeping for?' 'Alas!' said she, 'I must spin this straw into gold, and I know not how.' 'What will you give me,' said the hobgoblin, 'to do it for you?' 'My necklace,' replied the maiden.

He took her at her word, and sat himself down to the wheel, and whistled and sang:

> 'Round about, round about,
> Lo and behold!
> Reel away, reel away,
> Straw into gold!'

And round about the wheel went merrily; the work was quickly done, and the straw was all spun into gold.

When the king came and saw this, he was greatly astonished and pleased; but his heart grew still more greedy of gain, and he shut up the poor miller's daughter again with a fresh task.

What happens with the hobgoblin?

Why do you think the maiden agrees to the deal, even though it costs her a necklace?

What does the king think has happened?

Is the maiden honest about this? What effect does this have on what happens next?

Handout 4.11: Gray Area Analysis
Rumpelstiltskin by the Brothers Grimm

Name: _____

 **CONSIDER**: what does the text say?

 **CONNECT**: How does that connect to the focus skill?

Then she knew not what to do, and sat down once more to weep; but the dwarf soon opened the door, and said, 'What will you give me to do your task?' 'The ring on my finger,' said she.

So her little friend took the ring, and began to work at the wheel again, and whistled and sang:

> 'Round about, round about,
> Lo and behold!
> Reel away, reel away,
> Straw into gold!'

till, long before morning, all was done again.

 Has the miller's daughter lied? Or simply not told the whole truth?

 Has this gray area of honesty done more good or harm for the girl?

The king was greatly delighted to see all this glittering treasure; but still he had not enough: so he took the miller's daughter to a yet larger heap, and said, 'All this must be spun tonight; and if it is, you shall be my queen.'

As soon as she was alone that dwarf came in, and said, 'What will you give me to spin gold for you this third time?'

'I have nothing left,' said she. 'Then say you will give me,' said the little man, 'the first little child that you may have when you are queen.' 'That may never be,' thought the miller's daughter: and as she knew no other way to get her task done, she said she would do what he asked.

Round went the wheel again to the old song, and the manikin once more spun the heap into gold. The king came in the morning, and, finding all he wanted, was forced to keep his word; so he married the miller's daughter, and she really became queen.

 What offer does the king make the maiden now?

 What influence does this offer have on the maiden's choices?

Handout 4.11: Gray Area Analysis
Rumpelstiltskin by the Brothers Grimm

Name: _____

 CONSIDER: what does the text say?

CONNECT: How does that connect to the focus skill?

At the birth of her first little child she was very glad, and forgot the dwarf, and what she had said. But one day he came into her room, where she was sitting playing with her baby, and put her in mind of it. Then she grieved sorely at her misfortune, and said she would give him all the wealth of the kingdom if he would let her off, but in vain; till at last her tears softened him, and he said, 'I will give you three days' grace, and if during that time you tell me my name, you shall keep your child.'

Now the queen lay awake all night, thinking of all the odd names that she had ever heard; and she sent messengers all over the land to find out new ones. The next day the little man came, and she began with TIMOTHY, ICHABOD, BENJAMIN, JEREMIAH, and all the names she could remember; but to all and each of them he said, 'Madam, that is not my name.'

The second day she began with all the comical names she could hear of, BANDY-LEGS, HUNCHBACK, CROOK-SHANKS, and so on; but the little gentleman still said to every one of them, 'Madam, that is not my name.'

The third day one of the messengers came back, and said, 'I have travelled two days without hearing of any other names; but yesterday, as I was climbing a high hill, among the trees of the forest where the fox and the hare bid each other good night, I saw a little hut; and before the hut burnt a fire; and round about the fire a funny little dwarf was dancing upon one leg, and singing:

> '"Merrily the feast I'll make.
> Today I'll brew, tomorrow bake;
> Merrily I'll dance and sing,
> For next day will a stranger bring.
> Little does my lady dream
> Rumpelstiltskin is my name!"'

 How does the dwarf feel about taking away the queen's child?

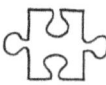 What do you think about his glee over his trick?

 How does the dwarf's name get revealed?

 What do you think about the queen sending messengers to sneak around the kingdom to avoid her fate?

Handout 4.11: Gray Area Analysis
Rumpelstiltskin by the Brothers Grimm

Name: _____

 CONSIDER: what does the text say?

 **CONNECT**: How does that connect to the focus skill?

When the queen heard this she jumped for joy, and as soon as her little friend came she sat down upon her throne, and called all her court round to enjoy the fun; and the nurse stood by her side with the baby in her arms, as if it was quite ready to be given up.

Then the little man began to chuckle at the thought of having the poor child, to take home with him to his hut in the woods; and he cried out, 'Now, lady, what is my name?'

'Is it JOHN?' asked she.

'No, madam!'

'Is it TOM?'

'No, madam!'

'Is it JEMMY?'

'It is not.'

'Can your name be RUMPELSTILTSKIN?' said the lady slyly.

'Some witch told you that!— some witch told you that!' cried the little man, and dashed his right foot in a rage so deep into the floor, that he was forced to lay hold of it with both hands to pull it out.

Then he made the best of his way off, while the nurse laughed and the baby crowed; and all the court jeered at him for having had so much trouble for nothing, and said, 'We wish you a very good morning, and a merry feast, Mr RUMPLESTILTSKIN!'

 Describe this third meeting between the dwarf and the queen.

 Why does the queen guess names when she already knows the truth?

 The queen made a deal with Rumpelstiltskin. Did she hold up her end of the bargain?

 Is it dishonest to make a deal and then refuse to follow through?

Handout 4.11: Rumpelstiltskin Reflection

Name: _____

Fill in the blanks to follow the chain of events in Rumpelstiltskin. Think about the reasons for deceit.

- The miller lied to the king because..

- The miller's daughter took credit for spinning the straw because…

- Rumpelstiltskin allowed the queen to take credit for his work because…

- The queen fooled Rumpelstiltskin about knowing his name because…

Why are people dishonest? Is it really lying if we are simply holding back information or not telling the whole truth?

Handout 4.12: Gray Area Analysis
Hansel and Gretel by the Brothers Grimm

Name: _____

 CONSIDER: what does the text say?

CONNECT: How does that connect to the focus skill?

Next to a great forest there lived a poor woodcutter with his wife and his two children. The boy's name was Hansel and the girl's name was Gretel. He had but little to eat, and once, when a great famine came to the land, he could no longer provide even their daily bread.

One evening as he was lying in bed worrying about his problems, he sighed and said to his wife, "What is to become of us? How can we feed our children when we have nothing for ourselves?"

"Man, do you know what?" answered the woman. "Early tomorrow morning we will take the two children out into the thickest part of the woods, make a fire for them, and give each of them a little piece of bread, then leave them by themselves and go off to our work. They will not find their way back home, and we will be rid of them."

"No, woman," said the man. "I will not do that. How could I bring myself to abandon my own children alone in the woods? Wild animals would soon come and tear them to pieces."

"Oh, you fool," she said, "then all four of us will starve. All you can do is to plane the boards for our coffins." And she gave him no peace until he agreed.

"But I do feel sorry for the poor children," said the man.

The two children had not been able to fall asleep because of their hunger, and they heard what the stepmother had said to the father.

Gretel cried bitter tears and said to Hansel, "It is over with us!"

"Be quiet, Gretel," said Hansel, "and don't worry. I know what to do."

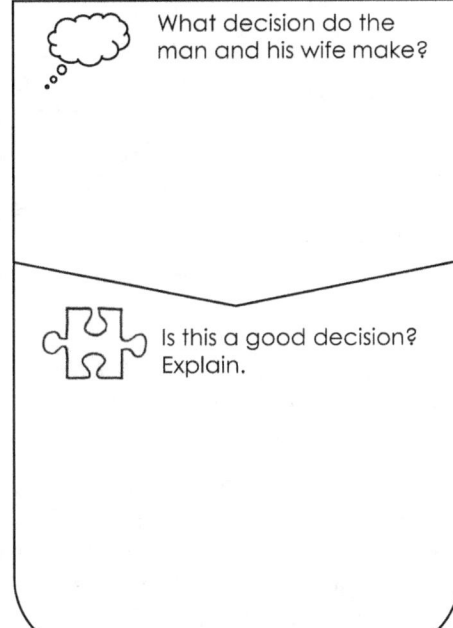

What decision do the man and his wife make?

Is this a good decision? Explain.

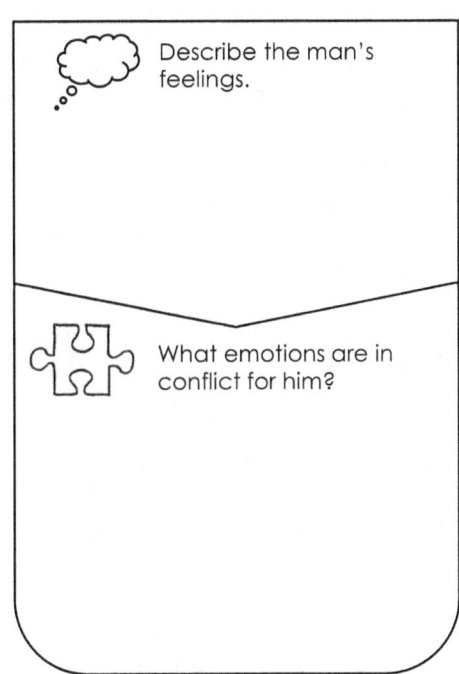

Describe the man's feelings.

What emotions are in conflict for him?

Handout 4.12: Gray Area Analysis
Hansel and Gretel by the Brothers Grimm

CONSIDER: what does the text say?

CONNECT: How does that connect to the focus skill?

Name: _____

> Starting here, highlight each time someone is dishonest.

And as soon as the adults had fallen asleep, he got up, pulled on his jacket, opened the lower door, and crept outside. The moon was shining brightly, and the white pebbles in front of the house were glistening like silver coins. Hansel bent over and filled his jacket pockets with them, as many as would fit.

Then he went back into the house and said, "Don't worry, Gretel. Sleep well. God will not forsake us." Then he went back to bed.

At daybreak, even before sunrise, the woman came and woke the two children. "Get up, you lazybones. We are going into the woods to fetch wood." Then she gave each one a little piece of bread, saying, "Here is something for midday. Don't eat it any sooner, for you'll not get any more."

Gretel put the bread under her apron, because Hansel's pockets were full of stones. Then all together they set forth into the woods. After they had walked a little way, Hansel began stopping again and again and looking back toward the house.

The father said, "Hansel, why are you stopping and looking back? Pay attention now, and don't forget your legs."

"Oh, father," said Hansel, "I am looking at my white cat that is sitting on the roof and wants to say good-bye to me."

The woman said, "You fool, that isn't your cat. That's the morning sun shining on the chimney."

However, Hansel had not been looking at his cat but instead had been dropping the shiny pebbles from his pocket onto the path.

When they arrived in the middle of the woods, the father said, "You children gather some wood, and I will make a fire so you won't freeze."

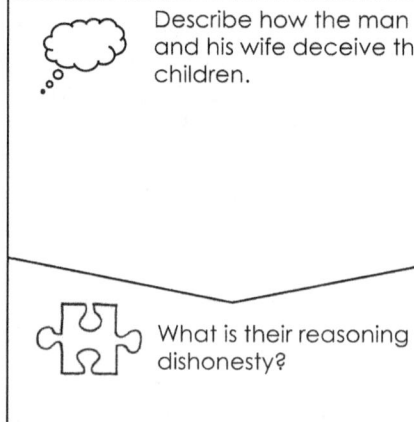

Describe how the man and his wife deceive the children.

What is their reasoning for dishonesty?

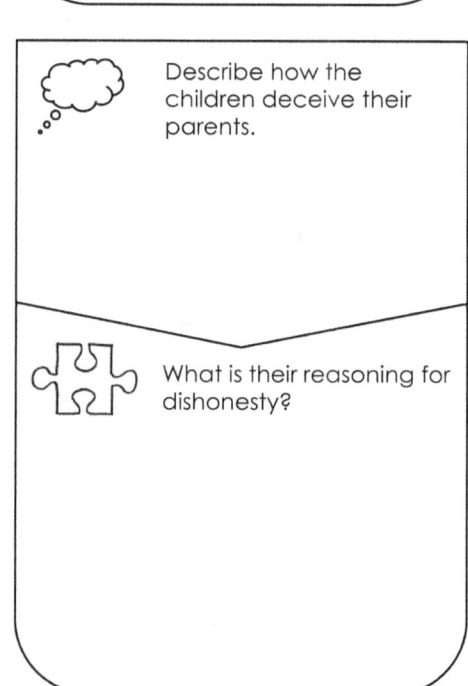

Describe how the children deceive their parents.

What is their reasoning for dishonesty?

2

Handout 4.12: Gray Area Analysis
Hansel and Gretel by the Brothers Grimm

Name: _____

 CONSIDER: what does the text say?

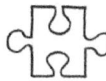 **CONNECT:** How does that connect to the focus skill?

Hansel and Gretel gathered together some twigs, a pile as high as a small mountain

The twigs were set afire, and when the flames were burning well, the woman said, "Lie down by the fire and rest. We will go into the woods to cut wood. When we are finished, we will come back and get you."

Hansel and Gretel sat by the fire. When midday came each one ate his little piece of bread. Because they could hear the blows of an ax, they thought that the father was nearby. However, it was not an ax. It was a branch that he had tied to a dead tree and that the wind was beating back and forth. After they had sat there a long time, their eyes grew weary and closed, and they fell sound sleep.

When they finally awoke, it was dark at night. Gretel began to cry and said, "How will we get out of woods?"

Hansel comforted her, "Wait a little until the moon comes up, and then we'll find the way."

After the full moon had come up, Hansel took his little sister by the hand. They followed the pebbles that glistened there like newly minted coins, showing them the way. They walked throughout the entire night, and as morning was breaking, they arrived at the father's house.

They knocked on the door, and when the woman opened it and saw that it was Hansel and Gretel, she said, "You wicked children, why did you sleep so long in the woods? We thought that you did not want to come back."

But the father was overjoyed when he saw his children once more, for he had not wanted to leave them alone.

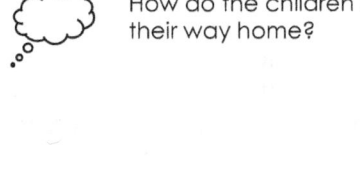

How do the children find their way home?

How is this related to the way they deceived their parents?

 What happens when the children arrive home?

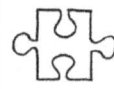 Describe the father's feelings about deceiving the children.

Handout 4.12: Gray Area Analysis
Hansel and Gretel by the Brothers Grimm

 CONSIDER: what does the text say?

 **CONNECT:** How does that connect to the focus skill?

Name: _____

Not long afterward there was once again great need everywhere, and one evening the children heard the mother say to the father, "We have again eaten up everything. We have only a half loaf of bread, and then the song will be over. We must get rid of the children. We will take them deeper into the woods, so they will not find their way out. Otherwise there will be no help for us."

The man was very disheartened, and he thought, "It would be better to share the last bit with the children."

But the woman would not listen to him, scolded him, and criticized him. He who says A must also say B, and because he had given in the first time, he had to do so the second time as well.

The children were still awake and had overheard the conversation. When the adults were asleep, Hansel got up again and wanted to gather pebbles as he had done before, but the woman had locked the door, and Hansel could not get out. But he comforted his little sister and said, "Don't cry, Gretel. Sleep well. God will help us."

Early the next morning the woman came and got the children from their beds. They received their little pieces of bread, even less than the last time. On the way to the woods, Hansel crumbled his piece in his pocket, then often stood still, and threw crumbs onto the ground.

"Hansel, why are you always stopping and looking around?" said his father. "Keep walking straight ahead."

"I can see my pigeon sitting on the roof. It wants to say good-bye to me."

"Fool," said the woman, "that isn't your pigeon. That's the morning sun shining on the chimney."

But little by little Hansel dropped all the crumbs onto the path. The woman took them deeper into the woods than they had ever been in their whole lifetime.

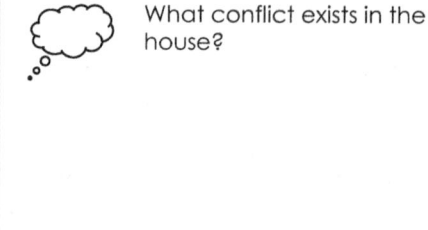

What conflict exists in the house?

How does this affect the father's decision?

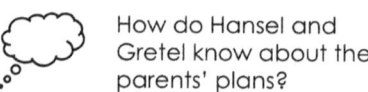

How do Hansel and Gretel know about the parents' plans?

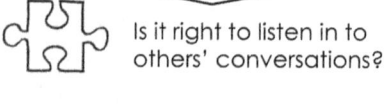

Is it right to listen in to others' conversations?

Handout 4.12: Gray Area Analysis
Hansel and Gretel by the Brothers Grimm

Name: _____

 **CONSIDER**: what does the text say?

CONNECT: How does that connect to the focus skill?

Once again a large fire was made, and the mother said, "Sit here, children. If you get tired you can sleep a little. We are going into the woods to cut wood. We will come and get you in the evening when we are finished."

When it was midday Gretel shared her bread with Hansel, who had scattered his piece along the path. Then they fell asleep, and evening passed, but no one came to get the poor children.

It was dark at night when they awoke, and Hansel comforted Gretel and said, "Wait, when the moon comes up I will be able to see the crumbs of bread that I scattered, and they will show us the way back home."

When the moon appeared they got up, but they could not find any crumbs, for the many thousands of birds that fly about in the woods and in the fields had pecked them up.

Hansel said to Gretel, "We will find our way," but they did not find it.

They walked through the entire night and the next day from morning until evening, but they did not find their way out of the woods. They were terribly hungry, for they had eaten only a few small berries that were growing on the ground. And because they were so tired that their legs would no longer carry them, they lay down under a tree and fell asleep.

It was already the third morning since they had left the father's house. They started walking again, but managed only to go deeper and deeper into the woods. If help did not come soon, they would perish. At midday they saw a little snow-white bird sitting on a branch. It sang so beautifully that they stopped to listen. When it was finished it stretched its wings and flew in front of them. They followed it until they came to a little house.

How does Hansel comfort Gretel?

Is he honest with her?

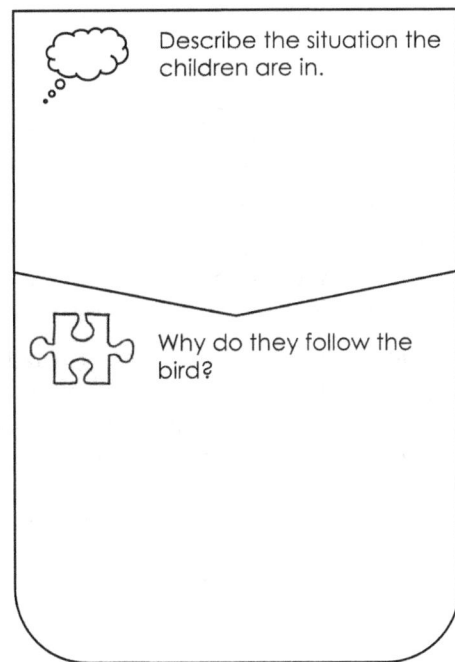

Describe the situation the children are in.

Why do they follow the bird?

Handout 4.12: Gray Area Analysis
Hansel and Gretel by the Brothers Grimm

 CONSIDER: what does the text say?

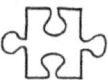 **CONNECT**: How does that connect to the focus skill?

Name: _____

The bird sat on the roof, and when they came closer, they saw that the little house was built entirely from bread with a roof made of cake, and the windows were made of clear sugar.

"Let's help ourselves to a good meal," said Hansel. "I'll eat a piece of the roof, and Gretel, you eat from the window. That will be sweet."

Hansel reached up and broke off a little of the roof to see how it tasted, while Gretel stood next to the windowpanes and was nibbling at them. Then a gentle voice called out from inside:

> Nibble, nibble, little mouse,
>
> Who is nibbling at my house?

The children answered:

> The wind, the wind,
>
> The heavenly child.

They continued to eat, without being distracted. Hansel, who very much like the taste of the roof, tore down another large piece, and Gretel poked out an entire round windowpane.

Suddenly the door opened, and a woman, as old as the hills and leaning on a crutch, came creeping out. Hansel and Gretel were so frightened that they dropped what they were holding in their hands.

But the old woman shook her head and said, "Oh, you dear children, who brought you here? Just come in and stay with me. No harm will come to you."

She took them by the hand and led them into her house. Then she served them a good meal: milk and pancakes with sugar, apples, and nuts. Afterward she made two nice beds for them, decked in white. Hansel and Gretel went to bed, thinking they were in heaven. But the old woman had only pretended to be friendly. She was a wicked witch who was lying in wait there for children. She had built her house of bread only in order to lure them to her, and if she captured one, she would kill him, cook him, and eat him; and for her that was a day to celebrate.

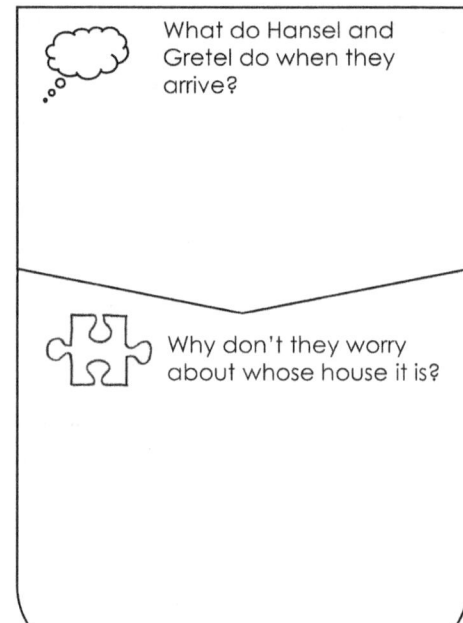

What do Hansel and Gretel do when they arrive?

Why don't they worry about whose house it is?

 How does the witch convince the children to come inside?

 Does this remind you of how another character was convinced to make a poor choice?

Handout 4.12: Gray Area Analysis
Hansel and Gretel by the Brothers Grimm

 CONSIDER: what does the text say?

 **CONNECT:** How does that connect to the focus skill?

Name: _____

Witches have red eyes and cannot see very far, but they have a sense of smell like animals, and know when humans are approaching.

When Hansel and Gretel came near to her, she laughed wickedly and spoke scornfully, "Now I have them. They will not get away from me again."

Early the next morning, before they awoke, she got up, went to their beds, and looked at the two of them lying there so peacefully, with their full red cheeks. "They will be a good mouthful," she mumbled to herself. Then she grabbed Hansel with her withered hand and carried him to a little stall, where she locked him behind a cage door. Cry as he might, there was no help for him.

Then she shook Gretel and cried, "Get up, lazybones! Fetch water and cook something good for your brother. He is locked outside in the stall and is to be fattened up. When he is fat I am going to eat him."

Gretel began to cry, but it was all for nothing. She had to do what the witch demanded. Now Hansel was given the best things to eat every day, but Gretel received nothing but crayfish shells.

Every morning the old woman crept out to the stall and shouted, "Hansel, stick out your finger, so I can feel if you are fat yet."

But Hansel stuck out a little bone, and the old woman, who had bad eyes and could not see the bone, thought it was Hansel's finger, and she wondered why he didn't get fat.

When four weeks had passed and Hansel was still thin, impatience overcame her, and she would wait no longer. "Hey, Gretel!" she shouted to the girl, "Hurry up and fetch some water. Whether Hansel is fat or thin, tomorrow I am going to slaughter him and boil him."

 How do the children trick the witch?

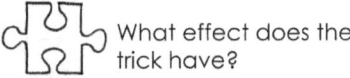 What effect does the trick have?

Handout 4.12: Gray Area Analysis
Hansel and Gretel by the Brothers Grimm

 CONSIDER: what does the text say?

 **CONNECT:** How does that connect to the focus skill?

Name: _____

Oh, how the poor little sister sobbed as she was forced to carry the water, and how the tears streamed down her cheeks! "Dear God, please help us," she cried. "If only the wild animals had devoured us in the woods, then we would have died together."

"Save your slobbering," said the old woman. "It doesn't help you at all."

The next morning Gretel had to get up early, hang up the kettle with water, and make a fire.

"First we are going to bake," said the old woman. "I have already made a fire in the oven and kneaded the dough."

She pushed poor Gretel outside to the oven, from which fiery flames were leaping. "Climb in," said the witch, "and see if it is hot enough to put the bread in yet." And when Gretel was inside, she intended to close the oven, and bake her, and eat her as well.

But Gretel saw what she had in mind, so she said, "I don't know how to do that. How can I get inside?"

"Stupid goose," said the old woman. The opening is big enough. See, I myself could get in." And she crawled up stuck her head into the oven.

Then Gretel gave her a shove, causing her to fall in. Then she closed the iron door and secured it with a bar. The old woman began to howl frightfully. But Gretel ran away, and the godless witch burned up miserably. Gretel ran straight to Hansel, unlocked his stall, and cried, "Hansel, we are saved. The old witch is dead."

Then Hansel jumped out, like a bird from its cage when someone opens its door. How happy they were! They threw their arms around each other's necks, jumped with joy, and kissed one another. Because they now had nothing to fear, they went into the witch's house. In every corner were chests of pearls and precious stones.

 Describe the events in this section.

 Have the children done anything wrong here?

Handout 4.12: Gray Area Analysis
Hansel and Gretel by the Brothers Grimm

Name: _____

 CONSIDER: what does the text say?

 **CONNECT**: How does that connect to the focus skill?

"These are better than pebbles," said Hansel, filling his pockets.

Gretel said, "I will take some home with me as well," and she filled her apron full.

"But now we must leave," said Hansel, "and get out of these witch-woods."

After walking a few hours they arrived at a large body of water. "We cannot get across," said Hansel. "I cannot see a walkway or a bridge."

"There are no boats here," answered Gretel, "but there is a white duck swimming. If I ask it, it will help us across."

Then she said,

> Duckling, duckling
> Here stand Gretel and Hansel.
> Neither a walkway nor a bridge,
> Take us on to your white back.

The duckling came up to them, and Hansel climbed onto it, then asked his little sister to sit down next to him.

"No," answered Gretel. "That would be too heavy for the duckling. It should take us across one at a time."

That is what the good animal did, and when they were safely on the other side, and had walked on a little while, the woods grew more and more familiar to them, and finally they saw the father's house in the distance. They began to run, rushed inside, and threw their arms around the father's neck.

The man had not had even one happy hour since he had left the children in the woods. However, the woman had died. Gretel shook out her apron, scattering pearls and precious stones around the room, and Hansel added to them by throwing one handful after the other from his pockets.

Now all their cares were at an end, and they lived happily together.

Now that the witch is gone, what do the children do?

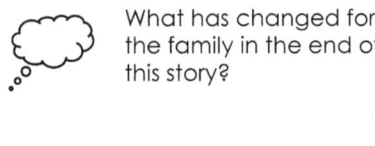

Are their actions honest? Ethical?

What has changed for the family in the end of this story?

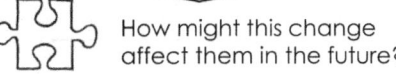

How might this change affect them in the future?

Handout 4.12: Hansel and Gretel Reflection

Name: _____

Fill in the blanks to follow the chain of events in Hansel and Gretel. Think about the reasons for deceit.

- The parents deceived the children because…

- The children deceived the parents because…

- The children deceived the witch because…

- The father was overjoyed when the children returned because…

- Why are people dishonest? Are there reasons that might make someone tell a lie or behave in tricky ways?

Sub-Skill 4

❏ Once students have completed their stories, guide groups in discussing the thinking questions on the last pages. Help them elaborate their thinking and tie their reasoning back to their stories. Key understandings for these questions can be found in Box 4.3.

TABLE 4.3
Puss in Boots Consider and Connect Outline

Story Page	Consider		Connect
Page 1	The youngest brother is left without an inheritance. He is very poor and alone in the world.	→	Because he is poor, hungry, and lonely, he is more likely to follow along with the cat's plans.
	The cat begins trying to earn the king's favor by catching game and giving it to the king.	→	The cat's behavior is a gray area—we don't know about the animals he is collecting; we do know it's not an entirely honest situation.
Page 2	The cat is fooling the king as well as his master.	→	The cat doesn't want to give away his plan to his master or the king.
	The cat has planned for this. He has gained favor with the king and hidden his master's clothing. He also knows when and where the king will pass.	→	The cat is clever, cunning, and a careful planner. He had a long-term plan from the beginning.
Page 3	The cat brings the Marquis into his lie by placing him in situations where he cannot tell the truth or he will be punished. He threatens field workers into lying for him.	→	The Marquis does not reveal the cat's tricks because he is enjoying their benefits. The workers do not tell on the cat because they are afraid.
	The Marquis goes along with the cat's tricks. He steps easily into the lie, although he does not verbally tell any lies himself.	→	This is not entirely truthful; even though he does not tell a lie himself, he is upholding the lies of the cat with his actions.
Page 4	The cat appeals to the ogre's hubris (ego) to get him to change form.	→	The cat was not entirely truthful; he tricked the ogre into changing form so that he could eat him and steal his castle and lands.
	The princess sees that the Marquis is wealthy, handsome, and charming, and falls in love.	→	The princess values appearances and comforts.

TABLE 4.4
The Emperor's New Clothes Consider and Connect Outline

Story Page	Consider		Connect
Page 1	The swindlers are dishonest, cunning, sly, and crafty. The emperor is vain, arrogant, and greedy.	→	Neither of these can be described in particularly positive terms.
	The emperor feels that he is very wise and powerful. He sees others as "lesser."	→	The emperor values appearances, fine clothing, and his own ego.
Page 2	The minister agrees with the swindlers and says he can see the cloth.	→	This is a gray area. Neither are necessarily ethical.
	The minister wants to protect his own image and his position in the court.	→	The minister values his position as well as his reputation more than honesty.
Page 3	The emperor doesn't question his advisors, even though he too cannot see the cloth.	→	The ministers are not truthful with him, so this trust appears misplaced.
	Compare and contrast: The ministers lie to maintain their positions as trusted advisors. The emperor lies because he is so vain and wants to believe in the fabulous cloth. They all lie because they don't want others to think they cannot see the cloth.		
Page 4	The noblemen all compliment the "clothes" that they cannot see.	→	Their values as a group are shared; each one has a group mentality.
	No one is truthful about the cloth on this page.	→	They are lying to others—they admit to themselves that they cannot see anything, but won't share that with anyone else.
Page 5	The emperor "regard[s] his costume with the greatest interest."	→	Others were still pretending just as he was. He wanted to be viewed as having something special.
	A child calls out the emperor.	→	The child values honesty above social norms. Also, the child is not an adult who feels they must conform to the ideas of others.

TABLE 4.5
Rumpelstiltskin Consider and Connect Outline

Story Page	Consider		Connect
Page 1	The miller and his daughter are simple country folk; the daughter is very beautiful.	→	The miller wants to improve his position in the world; his daughter is something he can brag about.
	The daughter finds herself locked in a dungeon with a task she cannot complete.	→	Her father's arrogance and dishonesty led to her being in this position.
Page 2	The hobgoblin offers to spin the straw into gold for the girl in exchange for her necklace.	→	She felt she had no other choices; she was in a desperate situation.
	The king thinks the girl has spun the straw into gold herself.	→	The maiden allows the king to believe this; this leads him to assign her a fresh pile of straw to spin.
Page 3	The miller's daughter has not outright lied, but she has withheld information and allowed others to draw their own conclusions.	→	Her actions have led her to be in a bigger predicament than she was in the first place.
	The offer from the king is that he will marry the girl if she can spin a third pile of straw to gold.	→	The maiden decides that she must do this task in order to get out of her situation in life.
Page 4	The dwarf is perfectly happy to take the queen's child away.	→	It's a little shocking that he would be so gleeful at separating a mother and child.
	The dwarf's arrogance in singing his name around a campfire is overheard by one of the queen's messengers.	→	The queen is trying to beat the dwarf at his own tricks by sneaking around. This is a gray area in terms of "fair play" and keeping promises.
Page 5	In the third and final meeting, the queen guesses several names before revealing that she knows the dwarf's name is Rumpelstiltskin.	→	She wants to trick him as she feels she has been tricked.
	She did not; she found ways to avoid holding up her end of the bargain.	→	This is a gray area. It does not seem fair, even though the bargain was a serious one. She got what she wanted, and the dwarf got nothing.

TABLE 4.6

Hansel and Gretel Consider and Connect Outline

Story Page	Consider		Connect
Page 1	The man and wife decide to abandon the children in the forest.	→	This decision means that they will not be left with nothing, but it is not a good decision for the children.
	The man doesn't want to abandon his children.	→	He wants to take care of his children, but he also doesn't want to starve. Self-preservation and love are in conflict.
Page 2	The man and his wife lie about their purpose for heading into the woods.	→	They don't want the children to protest; they want them to come along willingly.
	The children eavesdrop on their parents' plans and bring rocks to drop along their journey.	→	They don't want to get left behind in the forest.
Page 3	The children follow the path of dropped pebbles home.	→	They had dropped the pebbles in secret, without being caught.
	The man is elated when the children arrive home. The wife scolds them, pretending that they had not been left intentionally.	→	The father still feels guilty about the deception.
Page 4	The man and his wife do not have enough food to feed the family. They disagree about how to handle this shortage.	→	The father is torn between preserving his own life and the desire to keep his children in the home.
	Hansel and Gretel again eavesdrop on their parents' late-night conversations.	→	Eavesdropping is a gray area. While not polite or socially acceptable, in most instances it is not morally "wrong" to do so.
Page 5	Hansel says he has a plan for this journey as well.	→	He does not tell her all that he knows because he does not want her to be frightened.
	The children are lost in the woods and do not know which way to go.	→	They don't know what else to do, so they follow the bird because it seems to want them to do so.

(Continued)

TABLE 4.6
(Continued)

Story Page	Consider		Connect
Page 6	When Hansel and Gretel arrive at the cake house, they help themselves to a good meal.	→	They are very hungry and do not think about whose house they might be devouring.
	The witch convinces them to come inside by pretending to be kind and serving them a delicious meal.	→	The wife reassured the husband that no harm would come to the children in order to convince him to abandon them in the forest.
Page 7	The children take advantage of the witch's weaknesses (poor eyesight, greed) in order to trick her.	→	Hansel and Gretel are able to avoid being eaten by the witch by tricking her.
Page 8	In this section, the witch grows impatient with the children and decides to eat them. Gretel pretends not to understand how to use an oven, and when the witch moves to show her how to do it, Gretel pushes her in and burns her up.	→	The children killed the witch. Killing is not acceptable. If they hadn't killed the witch, however, they would have been eaten. This is a gray area.
Page 9	The children gather up as many jewels and treasures as they can carry and set off to find their way home.	→	They are technically stealing, although, with the witch gone, these objects might be considered as "found."
	The wife has died, leaving only the woodcutter. When the children arrive home with the jewels, they are no longer concerned with meager survival.	→	This can help them to be able to live more comfortably in the future.

Box 4.3: Fairytale Reflections Key Understandings

❏ *The Emperor's New Clothes*: The swindlers lied to the emperor because they wanted to get rich without doing any work. The advisors all lied to the emperor because they didn't want to appear stupid, nor did they want to be fired. The emperor decided to go out without any clothing because he was very vain, and assumed everyone else could see what he could not. The child told the truth because he was honest and didn't think about how his comments might hurt the emperor's feelings.

❏ *Rumpelstiltskin*: The miller lied to the king because he was proud; he wanted to show off his beautiful daughter. The miller's daughter took credit for spinning the straw because she wanted to get out of the situation she was in. Rumpelstiltskin allowed the queen to take credit for his work because he was being rewarded and still wanted to live his life in secrecy. The queen fooled Rumpelstiltskin about knowing his name because she wanted to play a trick on him like he had played on her.

❏ *Hansel and Gretel*: The parents deceive the children because they don't want them to try and stay in the house. The children deceive the parents because they value their safety and know the fate that awaits them if they are left alone in the forest. The children deceived the witch because they were able to take advantage of her weaknesses (eyesight) and greed in order to save themselves. The father was overjoyed when the children returned because he had felt great guilt about deceiving them in the first place.

❏ After students have completed their fairytales, bring the whole group back together and allow a few moments to share first impressions of each story. Then, direct students to Handout 4.9b (after reading). Scaffold support as students complete the questions on this handout, and then discuss reflections as a whole group.

❏ As a group, complete the statement "Honesty is the best policy. *Except...*"

Discussing Gray Area Authentic Application Activity: Socratic Seminar

Objective: Assign value to a real-world context, coming to consensus on what is most important when it comes to rules.

Materials

- ❏ *We Found a Hat* by Jon Klassen (teacher's copy)
- ❏ Handout 4.13: Socratic Seminar Preparation Page (one per student)

Whole Group Introduction

- ❏ Remind students of the gray area they found in their fairytales regarding honesty. Then, remind students of the gray area in choices they heard about with Solomon and Sheba.
- ❏ Have a discussion for a few moments—how does it feel to discuss the gray area? Are we always able to come to a single conclusion?

Read Aloud Activity

- ❏ Read aloud *We Found a Hat* by Jon Klassen. In this story, a pair of turtles find a single hat. As they decide what to do with it, they raise the gray areas of honesty, loyalty, and tricky decisions. As you read, think aloud and make connections to both the value questions (like in the fairytales) as well as the decision-making processes (like in *The Wisdom Bird*).

Authentic Application Activity

- ❏ Socratic Seminar is a teaching strategy that provides students the opportunity to discuss a topic or concept to gain a deeper understanding. Socrates believed that students learn best when provided the opportunity to come to an understanding themselves through thoughtful questioning. Socrates did not provide answers to his students' questions; rather, he responded to questions with more questions. This allowed the students to examine their own thinking and come to their own conclusions. This is the perfect authentic way to practice discussing gray area!

The Socratic Method
- ❏ Requires all students feel safe to contribute to the discussion; team-building must occur before attempting a seminar.
- ❏ Uses questions to examine values and beliefs focusing on moral education as well as information.

Handout 4.13: Socratic Seminar Preparation

Name: _____

The question for our Socratic Seminar discussion is:

Find evidence to support your thinking about this question.

EVIDENCE

EVIDENCE

EVIDENCE

Other points I want to raise:

My own opinions:

After our discussion, I think:

- ❏ Demands a classroom environment characterized by "productive discomfort."
- ❏ Is used to demonstrate complexity and uncertainty in our world.

Teacher's Role

- ❏ The teacher is the facilitator. The role of the teacher in a Socratic Seminar shifts from the "Sage on the Stage" to the "Guide on the Side." As the teacher, you must guide the students through further questioning and create a shared dialogue.
- ❏ Find a space where all students can face each other either moving their desks into a circle or sitting on the floor in a circle.
- ❏ Set dialogue guidelines. Participation requires students to be active listeners. Ask students to connect their statements with those before them using phrases like "I agree with...because..." or "I respectfully disagree with...because..." Remind students that they are encouraged to ask one another questions.
- ❏ Teach students about natural lulls in conversation and when it is appropriate to begin their next statement. Also talk about conversation "hogs" and "logs." A "hog" talks the entire time and doesn't allow others to speak. A "log" is someone who doesn't speak and allows the conversation to take place without their voice.
- ❏ Allow for wait time. Silence is not the enemy! Let students sit with a question for at least 10 seconds without rephrasing it. Students need time to grapple with challenging questions.
- ❏ Encourage students to take ownership of the conversation. Students should ask one another clarifying questions and feel comfortable asking the group a new question to further the discussion.
- ❏ The teacher may interject with either quick teaching moments, clarifying statements, or additional questions; however, this approach should be used with caution so as not to take over the dialogue. See Box 4.1 for some prompting questions to aid with stalls in discussion.

Box 4.1: Socratic Seminar Prompting Questions

- ❏ Who can offer a different perspective?
- ❏ Can you please support that statement with evidence from the text?
- ❏ Can you clarify your statement?

EVALUATIVE THINKING for Advanced Learners, Grades 3–5

- Who hasn't had a chance to speak yet?
- Has anyone had a change of heart?
- Who has changed their point of view?
- What piece of evidence made you change your opinion?
- Can anyone give a counter-argument?
- How can you relate this to your own life?
- Who else should read this piece? Why?
- Why is this information important?
- Do you agree or disagree with the author?
- What other evidence would you need to change your mind?
- What else can you tell us about … ?
- What makes you say/think … ?

Implementation

- Go over Socratic Seminar guidelines and expectations.

Box 4.2: Socratic Seminar Expectations

- *All participants must come prepared.*
    - Read the text(s) carefully.
    - Take notes.
    - Complete the Preparation Page.
- *Be an active participant and listener.*
    - Listen to what others say and don't interrupt.
    - Try to connect your idea to others.
    - "I agree with…because…"
    - "I respectfully disagree with…because…"
    - Ask clarifying questions when needed.
- *Speak clearly.*
    - State your opinion or idea in concise language.
    - Provide text evidence when possible.
    - Speak at a volume that works for our space and our group.
- *Be respectful.*
    - Speak only when it is your turn.
    - You don't have to raise your hand, but try not to interrupt others.
    - This is an exchange of ideas, not a debate.

❏ Allow students time to prepare. Distribute the Socratic Seminar Graphic Organizer (Handout 4.13) and allow students time to jot down their notes/ideas in the "I think…because…" section. Tell students they will have 10–15 minutes to gather their thoughts on the focus question. For the purpose of this Socratic Seminar, the teacher should choose a focus question that they feel their students will be able to respond to and discuss at length, given what they have read and their readiness levels. Possible focus questions are listed in Box 4.3.

> ### Box 4.3: Discussing Gray Area Socratic Seminar Focus Questions
>
> ❏ Are there times when we can bend our values for good reasons?
> ❏ How true is the proverb "Honesty is the best policy?"
> ❏ What is the most important value to stick to?
> ❏ How can we share our values with others?

Facilitate the Socratic Seminar. Position students in a circle facing one another and pose the focus question. Allow students to share their insights and discuss.

❏ After the seminar, provide a debrief of what you heard throughout the conversation. Summarize the main points to ensure learning. Finally, have students complete the final section on the Socratic Seminar graphic organizer (Handout 4.13).
❏ **Assessment:** Overall performance and deep thinking based on discussion participation and student thinking framework responses should be informally assessed throughout the unit. Rubrics are available in Appendix A.
  ■ **Socratic Seminar Rubric:** Quickly assess student participation and preparedness along a continuum to show growth.
  ■ **Socratic Seminar Self-Reflection:** Students evaluate their own participation and levels of thinking through the seminar process.

Discussing Gray Area Concluding Activities

❏ Distribute the Discussing Gray Area Exit Ticket (Appendix A). Ask students to reflect on their learning about the skill of Discussing Gray Area, and when it might be ok to discuss situations which do not have

a clear solution. Allow time for students to complete the exit ticket. Use this as a formative assessment to gain a better understanding of your students' readiness to effectively practice the skill.
- ❑ If desired, complete the Group Using Discussing Gray Area (Appendix A) to track students' progress with the skill.
- ❑ If desired, use the Evaluative Thinking Student Observation Rubric (Appendix A) to assess and quantify individual students' mastery.
- ❑ Ask students to retrieve their Evaluative Thinking Avatar (Handout I.4). In the Discussing Gray Area box, they should either record the main ideas about the thinking skill or illustrate their avatar using the skill of Discussing Gray Area.

Bibliography

Andersen, H.C. (1999). *Andersen's fairy tales.* https://www.gutenberg.org/ebooks/1597

Anonymous. (2007). *The frog prince and other stories.* https://www.gutenberg.org/ebooks/20437.

Grimm, J., and Grimm, W. (2001). *Grimm's fairy tales.* https://www.gutenberg.org/ebooks/2591.

Klassen, J. (2016). *We found a hat.* Somerville, MA: Candlewick Press.

Oberman, S. (2000). *The wisdom bird: A tale of Solomon and Sheba.* Honesdale, PA: Boyds Mill Press.

Perrault, C. (2010). *Puss in boots.* https://www.gutenberg.org/ebooks/31431.

CHAPTER 5

Sub-Skill 5

Making and Defending Judgments

TABLE 5.1
Making and Defending Judgments Sub-Skill Outline

	Thinking Skill Outline
Focus Questions	❏ How can we choose? ❏ Once we choose, how can we defend our choices?
Lesson 1	*Evaluating the Choices of Others* ❏ **Trade Book Focus:** *Mufaro's Beautiful Daughters* by John Steptoe ❏ **Practice Activity:** Introduction to the Evaluation Matrix: Analyzing the choices of others using a quantitative method.
Lesson 2	*Defending Our Own Choices* ❏ **Trade Book Focus:** *What Pet Should I Get?* by Dr. Seuss ❏ **Practice Activity:** Application of the Evaluation Matrix: Creating a matrix to make a choice of our own.
Authentic Application Activity	*The Best Toy* ❏ **Trade Book Focus:** *The Marvelous Toy* by Tom Paxton ❏ **Authentic Application:** Students will work through a decision-making process to make a judgment about the Best Toy Ever. They will defend this judgment before an audience of their peers.

Making and Defending Judgments Lesson 1: Evaluating the Choices of Others

Objective: Introduce the Evaluation Matrix to help students objectively evaluate decisions and potential solutions based on criteria and values. .

Materials

- Handout 5.1: Making and Defending Judgments Anchor Chart (one for display)
- *Mufaro's Beautiful Daughters* by John Steptoe (teacher's copy)
- Handout 5.2: Read Aloud Reflection (one per student)
- Handout 5.3: The King's Choice Evaluation Matrix (one per student)

Whole Group Introduction

- Tell students that they'll be working now to put together all of their evaluative thinking skills (*considering perspectives, developing criteria, assigning value,* and *gray area*) to make and defend their judgments. They will have to make choices and give their reasoning for what they choose.
- Review the Making and Defending Judgments Anchor Chart (Handout 5.1). Tell students that although many problems will not have a clear correct answer, we must still come to a conclusion. This means we have to make a decision, and we must be able to defend that decision using sound reasons.
- Pose the following: You have the choice to either buy a new bike or buy a new video game. You can have either one, but not both. What do you choose? Why is that your choice? Give students a few moments for silent reflection, and then have them turn and talk to a neighbor. They should share both their decision and why they chose what they did.
- Elicit a few volunteers to share their thinking. This is a fairly low-stakes choice; how did students make their decisions? Probe for justification.

Handout 5.1: Making and Defending Judgements Anchor Chart

MAKING & DEFENDING JUDGEMENTS

CHOOSING A SOLUTION AND GIVING REASONS FOR THAT CHOICE

EVALUATIVE THINKING for Advanced Learners, Grades 3–5

Read Aloud Activity

- ❏ Tell students that in the story you will read today, they will hear about a king who also has a tough choice ahead—he must choose a queen. Like in the choice between a bike and a video game, he has two seemingly good options: a man named Mufaro has two beautiful daughters!
- ❏ Read aloud from *Mufaro's Beautiful Daughters*. Pause to think aloud about how each daughter handles the trials placed before her. What choices does each make?
- ❏ Distribute the Read Aloud Reflection page (Handout 5.2). Work through these questions together and discuss responses. Key understandings for this read aloud are highlighted in Box 5.1.

Box 5.1: *Mufaro's Beautiful Daughters* Key Understandings

- ❏ *Story summary*: In this story, a king seeks a wife. In a nearby village, a man named Mufaro has two beautiful daughters. Each seeks to be the next queen. In traveling to meet the king, the nature of each daughter's character is revealed. In the end, the king chooses the daughter with the greatest strength of character based upon how she fared in a series of "tests" along her journey.
- ❏ *The king's judgment*: The king decides to base his decision on the care and kindness displayed by each of Mufaro's daughters.
- ❏ *The king's justification*: He justifies his decision based upon a series of "tests" he set out along the daughters' journey to the palace. The way that each daughter treated those who were considered "less than" showed her worthiness to be queen.
- ❏ *Mufaro's daughters*:
  - Manyara is ill-tempered, teases her sister, and is arrogant. She does not feel that it is important to be kind to others, even to her own family.
  - Nyasha is renowned for her kindness to others. She loves to work in the garden and is often found singing and helping others.
- ❏ The beauty of each daughter is revealed differently. While Manyara is outwardly beautiful, Nyasha demonstrates a kindness

Handout 5.2: Read Aloud Reflection
Mufaro's Beautiful Daughters by John Steptoe

Name: _____

Briefly summarize the story.

| What judgement does the king make? | How does the king justify his judgement? |

Describe each of Mufaro's daughters.

Even at the end, Mufaro says he has two "beautiful and worthy" daughters. Does the king agree with Mufaro's idea of what it means to be "beautiful and worthy"?

What does this story have to teach us about what it means to be beautiful?

> and caring spirit that indicates inner beauty as well. The king values inner beauty over outward beauty.
> ❏ The story teaches us that we are most beautiful when we demonstrate kindness.

Skill Development Activity

❏ **The Evaluation Matrix** is a tool designed to objectively evaluate multiple ideas using specific criteria in an object. It can be helpful to assign point values to the scoring in which to obtain a numerical evaluation of the possibilities, giving an unbiased result.

❏ The Evaluation Matrix strategy is useful when you have many ideas and want to weigh the value of each idea. This tool also helps when you want to evaluate all your options using relevant criteria. See Figure 5.1 for an overview.

❏ **Steps for Evaluation Matrix:**
  - List the options/ideas you want to evaluate on the left column going straight down.
  - Identify the criteria you will use to evaluate the options; record these as column headings.
  - Determine the rating scale to use when evaluating. I often use 1—low idea, 2—ok idea, 3—good idea, or 4—best idea. Be sure to carefully analyze the results. Consider high and low ratings, but don't limit yourself to only the highest total score. Look for combinations or ways to improve upon the options.
  - After rating the options/items, summarize the results as either *use now*, *modify*, or *reject*.
  - Analyze results and decide what to do next.

❏ **Applying the Evaluation Matrix:** Normally, you would begin by naming the options and criteria; however, for this lesson, these portions of the matrix have been completed for you so that students can get a feel for how this strategy works.

❏ Distribute Handout 5.3.

❏ Tell students that they will be analyzing the king's choice of a queen using a strategy called an Evaluation Matrix (see Figure 5.1). First, they will determine which criteria the king considered by completing the table at the top of the page. For each test the girls face, the king was seeking a particular value. Students should think about each test and the value being sought to develop the king's criteria.

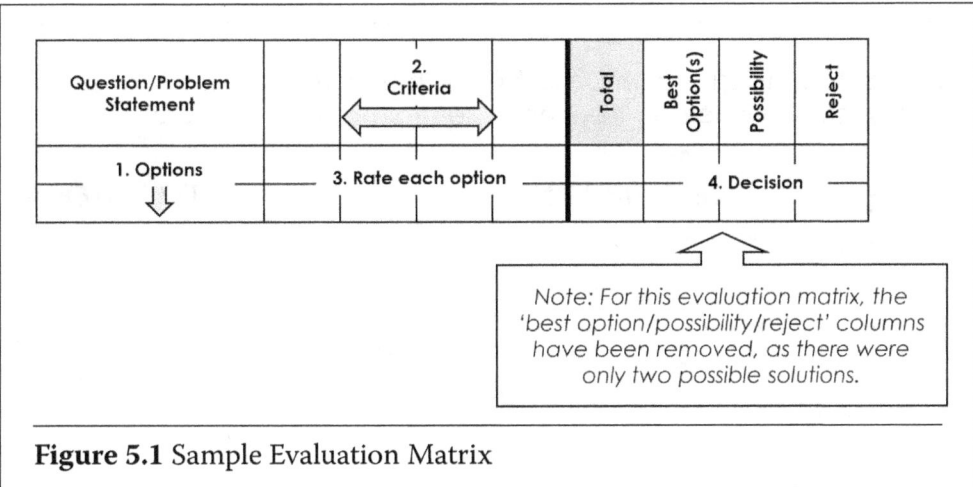

Figure 5.1 Sample Evaluation Matrix

- *The little boy*: The king is testing generosity. Manyara refuses to give the boy something to eat, while Nyasha gives the boy a yam unquestioningly.
- *The old woman*: The king is testing openness to the input of others. Manyara refuses to listen to advice; Nyasha doesn't question the woman's directions, but thanks her for her help with a small gift.
- *The trees*: The king is testing positivity of perspective. Manyara shouts and laughs at the trees, which seem to be laughing back at her. In contrast, the trees seem to bow down to Nyasha, who bows back to them.
- *The snake*: The king is testing courage. The snake appears to Manyara as a five-headed monster, and Manyara flees, frightened. To Nyasha, the snake is a garden snake she finds familiar to her from her garden patch at home; she is pleased to see her old friend.

❏ Once this table is completed, students should copy their criteria down into the criteria columns of the evaluation matrix.
❏ Move through each criterion rating the idea as follows: 1—low, 2—ok, 3—good, 4—better, and 5—best. Each criterion should be ranked for each girl, giving a rating to how well the girl demonstrated the target value.
❏ After rating the options, add the girls' totals. In what areas did one girl stand out above the other? Did the king make a good decision? Was it clear?
❏ Discuss with students: How did this matrix help make the king's decision and criteria very clear?
❏ Note that the evaluation matrix does not tell you specifically which option to choose but gives you a way of ranking/scoring options to help point you toward a solution that aligns with your set criteria. In this case, the king's set criteria pointed toward Nyasha as the queen, and this is what he chose.

Handout 5.3: The King's Choice

Name: _____

Think about the tests that the girls face. Describe each one from the story, and then think about what value or criteria it helped the king to see (or not see) in the girls.

TEST	DESCRIPTION	VALUE/CRITERIA
little boy		
old woman		
trees		
snake		

Are there any other criteria you think would be important that are missing from these tests?

Now, use the EVALUATION MATRIX to help you analyze how the king made his choice.
1. Fill in the criteria tested by each trial the girls faced.
2. Rate the girls in each criteria category from 1-5 (1 being lowest scoring, and 5 being highest scoring). Think about how well the girl did on that particular test/criteria.
3. Add up the girls' scores across the criteria. Then, answer the question: Who is the most worthy future queen?

POSSIBLE SOLUTIONS / CRITERIA	Physical Beauty (Appearance)	Little Boy:	Old Woman:	Trees:	Snake:	Total
NYASHA						
MANYARA						

Who is the best future queen? How do you know?

Sub-Skill 5

Making and Defending Judgments Lesson 2: Defending Our Own Choices

Objective: Apply the Evaluation Matrix strategy to a personal decision.

Materials

- *What Pet Should I Get?* By Dr. Suess (teacher's copy)
- Handout 5.4: Read Aloud Reflection (one per student)
- Handout 5.5: Pet Considerations (one per student)
- Handout 5.6a–f: Pet Possibility Posters (one of each, enlarged or duplicated for a gallery walk)
- Handout 5.7: Choosing a Pet Evaluation Matrix (one per student)
- Handout 5.8: My Perfect Pet Presentation Page (one per student)

Whole Group Introduction

- Remind students that in the previous lesson, they worked to apply the Evaluation Matrix to someone else's decision. In this lesson, they'll apply the Evaluation Matrix to develop their own criteria and make their own choice.
- Pose the following question: "Suppose that our school had used too many snow days and we needed to make up a few days of school. You have to choose: would you rather come to school one Saturday a month for the last 4 months of school *or* extend the school year by 4 days, cutting into summer break?"
- Discuss the following with students: What are the pros and cons of each choice? What criteria would we use to choose? What do we value more: Saturdays or summer break? What would we choose? How could we defend our choice to those who disagree?

Read Aloud Activity

- Tell students that you'll be reading aloud a book today about a kid who needs to make a tough choice. As you read, ask students to look out for the criteria that the child discusses, as well as what they value.
- Read aloud *What Pet Should I Get?* pausing to help students note criteria (what dad says, number of pets, size of home, etc.), perspective

taking (what the sister says matters too!), and values (what is most important in a pet?).
- ❏ When you finish reading, complete the Read Aloud Reflection page (Handout 5.4), asking students to predict what kind of pet they ended up getting! Key understandings for the read aloud are outlined in Box 5.2.

> ### Box 5.2: *What Pet Should I Get?* Key Understandings
>
> ❏ *Story conflict summary*: This story centers around a brother and sister who are sent to the pet store to choose a pet. With so many options, they have a hard time deciding what to bring home!
> ❏ *Considerations*: The kids have to pick a single pet. They consider:
>   - The size of their house
>   - The activity level of the pet
>   - The pet's habitat (not in a tent)
> ❏ *Pets ruled out*: A "yent," a fast pet, a large pet.
> ❏ *Pet possibilities*: Dogs, cats, rabbits, birds, fish.

Skill Development Activity

- ❏ Tell students they will be choosing their family's next pet through analyzing various options and developing criteria.
- ❏ Distribute the Pet Considerations sheet (Handout 5.5). Students will review the information on considerations to choose pets. They should jot down their own personal considerations on this page.
- ❏ Hang the Pet Profile pages (Handout 5.6a–f) around the room and guide students on a "gallery walk" to discover several types of pets. Students should move in small groups or pairs around to the various pages, taking notes on pet options they find interesting.
- ❏ Distribute the Evaluation Matrix sheet (Handout 5.7). Guide students in developing criteria for the best pet for their family. Note that students may have different types of criteria, and that is ok! Each student will be deciding for themselves, and must create criteria that reflect their own values, ideals, and situations.

Handout 5.4: Read Aloud Reflection
What Pet Should I Get? by Dr. Seuss

Name: _____

What was the conflict in the story?

What kids' considerations (criteria)?

What kinds of pets are ruled out?	What kind of pets remain possibilities?	What pet do you predict they got? Why?

Handout 5.5: Pet Considerations

Name: _____

So, you want to get a pet?

Good for you! Pets are a great joy and can be fun playmates. Before you get a pet, though, there are several things you need to consider.

- Think about your house. How much space do you have? Would it be ok if things got a little messy or got pet hair on them? Do you have enough space for a large pet, or should you think smaller? Do you need or have a fenced yard for outside play?
- Then, think about your family members. Does anyone have allergies? How much time do you have to spend with a pet? Can you take it for walks, clean it, keep its space clean, feed it, and spend time with it?
- You should also consider costs. Some pets are not too expensive to buy but might cost more to keep. Think about what equipment you'd need for a pet as well: do you need a dog bed? Fish tank? What about a veterinarian?
- Last, think about what kind of pet would make you happy to have in your home. When you choose a pet, you are choosing a companion! Choose wisely!

MY CONSIDERATIONS	GALLERY WALK: PET NOTES

Handout 5.6a: Types of Pets Gallery Walk

BIRD

GREAT FOR:	• People who want a pet that can do tricks • People who want an indoor pet
LESS GREAT FOR:	• Those who are gone for long stretches • People who want a quiet pet (birds can be noisy!)
NEEDS:	• Companion (either bird or human) • Cage or enclosure • Perch/toys • Light and space to fly and climb
EATS:	• Bird feed • Some fruit, seeds, nuts
COSTS:	• Average first year cost: ~$300 • Average lifetime cost: ~$3000 Note: larger birds can be *much* more expensive, costing over $5000 for the bird alone.
FAST FACTS:	• Average lifespan is 10-15 years • Come in lots of sizes, from ~4"-~40" • Outside birds (like chickens) need to be protected from predators • Cannot be house trained, so cages must be cleaned regularly

Handout 5.6b: Types of Pets Gallery Walk

CAT

GREAT FOR:	• Those who want a quiet pet that they can cuddle • Those who want a fairly low-maintenance pet
LESS GREAT FOR:	• Those with allergies • Those who don't want things in their home to have fur/get scratched
NEEDS:	• Litterbox (must clean daily) • Toys • Things to scratch • A designated space
EATS:	• Cat food (wet/canned or dry/kibble)
COSTS:	• Average first year cost: ~$1,800 • Average lifetime cost: ~$20,000
FAST FACTS:	• Cats can live up to 20 years • Cats can have distinct and fun personalities • Cats must be groomed regularly • Cats may not do well with smaller pets (like hamsters)

Handout 5.6c: Types of Pets Gallery Walk

DOG

GREAT FOR:
- Those with active lifestyles
- Those who want a pet to cuddle

LESS GREAT FOR:
- Those with allergies
- Those who want a low-maintenance and/or quiet pet

NEEDS:
- Exercise
- Companionship
- Leash/collar
- Space to run and play safely

EATS:
- Dog food (wet/canned or dry/kibble)

COSTS:
- Average first year cost: ~$2,000
- Average lifetime cost: ~$15,000

FUN FACTS:
- Dogs on average live 10-15 years
- Dog breeds can have varied and distinct personalities
- Dogs can be trained to do a variety of tricks
- Dogs must be groomed regularly

Handout 5.6d: Types of Pets Gallery Walk

FISH

GREAT FOR:
- Those who want a low maintenance pet
- Those who don't have a lot of space

LESS GREAT FOR:
- Those who travel often
- Those who want a pet to cuddle or play with

NEEDS:
- Fishbowl/aquarium (including accessories)
- Water treatment products/filter to keep habitat clean

EATS:
- Fish food

COSTS:
- *Varies greatly between fresh water and saltwater fish! Expect fish in a saltwater aquarium to be MUCH more expensive than a goldfish.*
- For goldfish, average first year cost: ~$250; average lifetime cost: ~$450

FAST FACTS:
- Goldfish can live up to 20 years!
- Saltwater fish must be chosen carefully; they do not all play well together
- Tank water must be carefully cleaned and kept at the right temperature and chemical balance for fish to thrive.

Handout 5.6e: Types of Pets Gallery Walk

RABBIT

GREAT FOR:	• Those who want a pet to play with and cuddle • Those with time to invest in care
LESS GREAT FOR:	• Families with young children • Those who want a low-maintenance pet
NEEDS:	• Safe, clean, and comfortable enclosure • Room to run and play • Toys to keep them busy
EATS:	• Grass/hay • Green leafy vegetables
COSTS:	• Average initial cost: ~$400 • Average lifetime cost: ~$10,000
FAST FACTS:	• Average rabbit lifespan is 7-10 years • Rabbits come in lots of sizes, from about 2 lbs to about 20 lbs • Rabbits are social and prefer to be around other rabbits

Handout 5.6f: Types of Pets Gallery Walk

TURTLE

GREAT FOR:
- Those with limited space or who prefer a lower-maintenance pet
- Those who enjoy watching a pet

LESS GREAT FOR:
- Those who prefer an interactive/cuddly pet
- Families with small children

NEEDS:
- Aquarium with proper habitat accessories (water environment, land environment); tank requires regular cleaning
- UV lamp/light

EATS:
- Leafy greens
- Limited amounts of insects or shrimp

COSTS:
- Average initial cost: ~$1,000
- Average yearly cost: ~$250

FAST FACTS:
- Turtles have a long lifespan and can live up to 50 years or more!
- Turtles can be carriers of salmonella (a bacteria that can make people sick), so good hand hygiene is important
- Turtles can grow anywhere from 4"-20" in length

Handout 5.7: Choosing a Pet Evaluation Matrix

Name: _____

What Pet Should You Get?

Use the evaluation matrix below to determine which is the best pet for your family.

1. Write your top four possible solutions in the first column. Then, list your criteria at the top of the next columns.
2. Go through each car and rate it against the criteria from 1- low, 2- ok, 3-good, or 4-best. Be sure to carefully analyze the results. Look for combinations or ways to improve upon the options.
3. After rating the options classify each of your possible solutions as either great option, possibility, or reject.

POSSIBLE SOLUTIONS \ CRITERIA →						Total	Great Option	Possibility	Reject

What pet will you get? Why?

Create a poster to convince your parents that you should get a pet. Write a paragraph defending the pet you choose for your family. Be sure to include the criteria used in your determination to defend your choice!

Handout 5.8: My Perfect Pet

Name: _____

- ❏ Guide students to work through each criterion, rating the idea as follows: 1—low, 2—ok, 3—good, or 4—best.
- ❏ Remind students to be sure to carefully analyze the results. Look for combinations or ways to improve upon the options.
- ❏ After rating the options, summarize the results as either "best options," "possibility," or "reject."
- ❏ Once students have made a decision, distribute the My Perfect Pet Presentation Page (Handout 5.8). Give students time to draw a picture of their perfect pet, and write a paragraph below to describe how they chose their pet and why it is perfect for them.
- ❏ Save time for students to share their decisions. What helped them make their choice? Was anyone's choice unclear even after using the matrix?

Making and Defending Judgments Authentic Application Activity: Making and Defending a Choice

Objective: Make and defend a choice in an authentic context.

Materials

- ❏ Handout 5.9: Toy Sort (one per small group)
- ❏ Chart Paper
- ❏ *The Marvelous Toy* by Tom Paxton (teacher's copy)
- ❏ Handout 5.10: Toy Show and Share (one per student)
- ❏ Handout 5.11: Toy Scavenger Hunt (one per student)
- ❏ Devices for students to access Toys Webmix
    - ■ Webmix Link: https://bit.ly/3dmv2Q5
    - ■ If you are not able to access the weblink or would prefer a non-digital option, gather a collection of articles and books about toys over time (what has been popular in the past, how toys have changed/developed over time, what makes toys popular, etc.)
- ❏ Handout 5.12: Best Toy Criteria Sheet (one per student)
- ❏ Handout 5.13: Best Toy Evaluation Matrix (one per student)
- ❏ Handout 5.14: Best Toy Judgment Sheet (one per student)

Whole Group Introduction

- ❏ Tell students that today they will be working to determine what is the best toy ever. Ask students to consider what toys they know of and elicit

EVALUATIVE THINKING for Advanced Learners, Grades 3–5

- responses. Then, distribute the Toy Sort cards (Handout 5.9) to small groups of students. Direct students to cut the cards apart, and clarify for them what each toy is if they are not familiar with it.
- Ask students to complete an open sort, placing the toys in groups and labeling their categories. Give students some time to work.
- After some work time, ask students to share:
  - What were their categories?
  - What toys fit in which groups?
  - Were there any toys that were hard to group? Why?
  - Could they add any other toys (not already listed) to any of their groups?
- Record the categories students generate on the board or an anchor chart for reference later. Possible categories of toys might include *outdoor/active, pretend play, building, games and puzzles, dolls/action figures, creative, plush, crafts, musical instruments, sports, vehicles, pre-school/baby,* or *electronics*. It is not necessary to use all of these suggested categories, but these ideas can be useful in helping guide discussion.

Read Aloud Activity

- Read aloud *The Marvelous Toy* by Tom Paxton. Note that in this story, the actual toy is never revealed; we don't see what it is.
- After reading, ask students: What was it that made the toy marvelous? What toys would you describe as marvelous?

Authentic Application Activity

- Distribute Handout 5.10. Invite students to participate in a Toy Show and Share: Give students time to draw their own favorite toy (you may choose to allow students to bring in a favorite toy as well, depending on your group). Each student should illustrate and write about their favorite toy. Allow time for sharing in small groups or partners. Remind students that they should share what makes their toy their favorite. What are the main characteristics that make it fun? Why do they like it? Would this toy be a favorite for everyone? Once students have shared, post favorite toys around the room and ask students to go on a gallery walk, looking at others' favorite toys and reading about what makes each toy a favorite. Then discuss: What did these toys have in common? What attributes made the toys our favorites?

Handout 5.9: Toy Sort

HULA HOOP	SILLY PUTTY	EASY BAKE OVEN
YO-YO	ETCH-A-SKETCH	GAME BOY
TRANSFORMERS	HOT WHEELS	RUBIK'S CUBE
SLINKY	G.I. JOE	JIGSAW PUZZLE
BARBIE	CABBAGE PATCH DOLLS	BALL
MR. POTATO HEAD	LEGOS	FRISBEE

Handout 5.9, continued: Toy Sort

BOARD GAMES	IPOD	TRAIN SET
SUPER SOAKER	RADIO FLYER WAGON	SOCK MONKEY
NERF	BEANIE BABIES	JUMP ROPE
PLAY DOH	CRAYONS	ERECTOR SET
COZY COUPE	BLOCKS	LINCOLN LOGS
TICKLE ME ELMO	VIEWFINDER	MARBLES

Handout 5.10: Favorite Toy Show and Share

Name: _____

MY FAVORITE TOY

- Next, students will participate in a Toy Scavenger Hunt. Students will visit the Toys Webmix (https://bit.ly/3dmv2Q5) or interact with a variety of teacher-curated materials about the subject of toys over time. They should explore the links to articles about toys, and watch a video or two there. You may choose to show more than one video if you'd like, although at least one is quite lengthy. As students explore, they should record their findings on the Toy Scavenger Hunt Recording Sheet (Handout 5.11). After some time exploring, discuss findings with students. What was interesting? New? Noteworthy?
- The next step will be developing criteria. Distribute the Best Toy Criteria Sheet (Handout 5.12). In pairs, students will work to develop criteria to help them decide what the Best Toy Ever is. Ask students to consider carefully the considerations for what makes a toy great, working through the sheet one piece at a time. Students should develop five total criteria. Then, pairs should team into groups of four to discuss and generate a list of possible "best toys." This list is unlimited in length. Finally, students should independently circle five toys from their list of possibilities to consider as possible best toys.
- Next, students will complete a Best Toy Evaluation Matrix: Guide students in working through the Evaluation Matrix (Handout 5.13), using their criteria and possibilities from the previous step. As students rate each choice, remind them to pay close attention to each criterion as it relates to each toy specifically. Help students to remain unbiased; just because they love a certain toy does not mean it will rate highly on every criterion! After rating each toy, students will add up the totals. Then, they will rate each choice as a *great option*, *possibility*, or *reject*. Finally, students will consider their matrix in making a judgment. Note: just because a toy scores the highest overall does *not* mean that it will necessarily be the clear winner. Students may choose a toy as the "best" even if it did not score the highest if they value one or another criterion more heavily. Help students to see this gray area and use the criteria and value to make their judgment.
- Finally, students will make a fairy tale of the Best Toy. Using both their Evaluation Matrix and their own judgment, students will choose a single toy to be ruled the best. Distribute the Best Toy Judgment Sheet (Handout 5.14). Students will record, illustrate, and explain their reasoning for their choice. You may also choose to have students illustrate their "Best Toy" on a separate sheet for display.
- Sharing and Discussion: Allow time for sharing and discussion. Ask probing questions, such as the following:
    - Were some criteria actually more important to you than others?
    - Where do we agree? Disagree?

Handout 5.11: Toy Scavenger Hunt

Name: _____

1. Visit the toys webmix: https://bit.ly/3dmv2Q5
2. Explore the links and videos.
3. Record your findings.

What are some of the oldest toys that were invented?	What are some categories that toys can be organized into?
What are some of the most popular toys ever?	What were some of the coolest toys you saw?
What toys did you recognize? Were there any that were new to you?	What other interesting facts/ideas did you find?

Handout 5.12: Best Toy Criteria

Name: _____

What are some categories of toys?

+

What is the main function of a toy?

+

What characteristics make a toy fun?

=

What are some CRITERIA that must be present for a toy to be "GREAT"? (Choose five criteria!)

Discuss and then record: What are some toys that are GREAT and could be "the best toy ever"?

Circle your top five options!

Handout 5.13: Best Toy Evaluation Matrix

Name: _____

What toy is the best?

1. Use the Evaluation Matrix below to help you decide which toy is the best.
2. First, write your criteria into the columns.
3. Then, fill in your top five toy possibilities into the rows.
4. Go through each toy and rate it against the criteria from 1- low, 2- ok, 3-good, or 4-best. Be sure to carefully analyze the results. Look for combinations or ways to improve upon the options.
5. After rating the options summarize the results as either great option, possibility, or reject.

	CRITERIA →					Total	Great Option	Possibility	Reject
POSSIBLE SOLUTIONS ↓									

Think about it: Even if one option has the highest score, it might not be the winner! Describe your thoughts.

What is your winner?

Handout 5.14: Best Toy Judgement

Name: _____

The BEST TOY EVER is...

Things that make it the best:

Draw the toy:

Its most important characteristics:

Describe this toy:

How I know it's the best:

- ■ Could we come up with a class consensus on a best toy? Or a best category of toys?
- ■ How did the evaluation matrix help us?
- ■ What was surprising or new?
- ■ Did any toys that we thought were great at the beginning not get rated as well as we would have predicted? Why?
❏ Display student presentation pages of "Best Toys," if possible.

Making and Defending Judgments Concluding Activities

❏ Distribute the Making and Defending Judgments Exit Ticket (Appendix A). Ask students to reflect on their learning about the skill of Making and Defending Judgments as well as strategies that can help them arrive at defensible solutions. Allow time for students to complete the exit ticket. Use this as a formative assessment to gain a better understanding of your students' readiness to effectively practice the skill.
❏ If desired, complete the Group Making and Defending Judgments (Appendix A) to track students' progress with the skill.
❏ If desired, use the Evaluative Thinking Student Observation Rubric (Appendix A) to assess and quantify individual students' mastery.
❏ Ask students to retrieve their Evaluative Thinking Avatar (Handout I.4). In the Making and Defending Judgments box, they should either record the main ideas about the thinking skill or illustrate their avatar using the skill of Making and Defending Judgments.

Bibliography

Paxton, T. (2009). *The marvelous toy*. New York: Penguin Random House.
Steptoe, J. (1989). *Mufaro's beautiful daughters*. New York: Scholastic Publishing.
Suess, D. (2015). *What pet should we get?* New York: Random House.

Appendix A
Assessments

Several assessment options are provided in this unit. It is not necessary to use all of the provided options; rather, you should choose the options that work best for your own classroom needs.

One aspect to pay close attention to is the indicators associated with each thinking skill. These indicators provide an outline of expected behavioral outcomes for students. As you work through the lessons, keep an eye out for students who are able to achieve the indicators efficiently and effectively, as well as those who may need more support. The intent of this unit is to foster a mastery mindset; make note of student growth and skill development as you progress, rather than focusing on summative outcomes against specific benchmarks.

1. **Exit Tickets:** Exit tickets are provided to correspond with each sub-skill. These are intended to be formative, giving you a sense of students' mastery and self-efficacy with each skill. These tickets will also give you great insight into areas where a re-visit is warranted. If a student would benefit from additional instruction in a sub-skill area, consider using one or more of the extension options listed in Appendix B.
2. **Individual Student Observations:** This form is intended for use for each student individually. All five thinking skills are outlined on the page, and you can track individual student progress toward indicator

goals easily. Use this form to gather data, report data to stakeholders, or simply help students see their own progress.

3. **Evaluative Thinking Sub-Skill Group Observation Checklists:** This checklist is provided for each thinking skill. This is a great running measure of students' mastery of the indicators associated with each thinking skill. Each skill has three indicators for mastery, and you can track student progress toward these goals as a group using this form.

4. **Socratic Seminar Assessment:** Provided here is a rubric for assessment after completion of Socratic Seminar. Also included is a form for students to self-evaluate their performance in this unique learning experience.

Handout A.1: Perspectives Exit Ticket

Name: _____
Date: _____

Considering perspectives means…

The easiest part about considering perspectives is…

The trickiest part about considering perspectives is…

How confident I feel about considering perspectives:

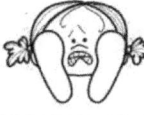   

Your opinion (feelings, questions, ideas, favorite parts) of this unit:

Handout A.2: Developing Criteria Exit Ticket

Name: _____
Date: _____

Developing criteria is…

The easiest part about developing criteria is…

The trickiest part about developing criteria is…

How confident I feel about developing criteria:

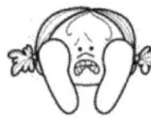   

Your opinion (feelings, questions, ideas, favorite parts) of this unit:

Handout A.3: Assigning Value Exit Ticket

Name: _____
Date: _____

Assigning value is…

The easiest part about assigning value is…

The trickiest part about assigning value is…

How confident I feel about assigning value:

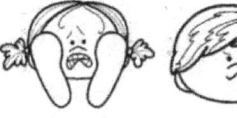

Your opinion (feelings, questions, ideas, favorite parts) of this unit:

Handout A.4: Gray Area Exit Ticket

Name: _____
Date: _____

Gray area is…

The easiest part about gray area is…

The trickiest part about gray area is…

How confident I feel about discussing gray areas:

Your opinion (feelings, questions, ideas, favorite parts) of this unit:

Handout A.5: Judgements Exit Ticket

Name: _____
Date: _____

Making & Defending Judgements is…

The easiest part about Making & Defending Judgements is…

The trickiest part about Making & Defending Judgements is…

How confident I feel about Making & Defending Judgements:

Your opinion (feelings, questions, ideas, favorite parts) of this unit:

Handout A.6: Individual Student Observation Rubric

Masterful	Exceeds expectations
Proficient	Independent mastery
Developing	Success with scaffolding
Beginning	Not yet achieved

Student name:

	MASTERFUL (4)	PROFICIENT (3)	DEVELOPING (2)	BEGINNING (1)
CONSIDERING PERSPECTIVES • Recognize alternate viewpoints • Evaluate how personal perspectives affect others • Consider various perspectives in constructing solutions	Notes:			
DEVELOPING CRITERIA • Determine which considerations are applicable • Analyze constraints in criteria • Develop criteria to align with a problem	Notes:			
ASSIGNING VALUE • Determine the core values of an idea or object • Evaluate orders of importance for groups of ideas or characteristics • Develop solutions based on core values	Notes:			
GRAY AREA • Recognize and summarize opposing viewpoints • Analyze areas of ambiguity • Evaluate solutions both objectively and subjectively	Notes:			
MAKING & DEFENDING JUDGEMENTS • Base judgements on evidence and values • Evaluate judgements based on criteria • Defend solutions thoroughly	Notes:			

Handout A.7: Considering Perspectives Group Checklist

*	Exceeds expectations
+	Independent mastery
✓	Success with scaffolding
o	Not yet achieved

Students	Indicators		
	Recognizes alternate viewpoints	Evaluate how personal perspectives affect others	Consider various perspectives in constructing solutions

Handout A.8: Developing Criteria Group Checklist

*	Exceeds expectations
+	Independent mastery
✓	Success with scaffolding
o	Not yet achieved

Students	Indicators		
	Determine which considerations are applicable	Analyze constraints in criteria	Develop criteria to align with a problem

Handout A.9: Assigning Value Group Checklist

*	Exceeds expectations
+	Independent mastery
✓	Success with scaffolding
o	Not yet achieved

Students	Indicators		
	Determine the core values of an idea or object	Evaluate orders of importance for groups of ideas or characteristics	Develop solutions based on core values

Handout A.10: Discussing Gray Area Group Checklist

*	Exceeds expectations
+	Independent mastery
✓	Success with scaffolding
o	Not yet achieved

Students	Indicators		
	Recognize and summarize opposing viewpoints	Analyze areas of ambiguity	Evaluate solutions both objectively and subjectively

Handout A.11: Making and Defending Judgements Group Checklist

*	Exceeds expectations
+	Independent mastery
✓	Success with scaffolding
o	Not yet achieved

Students	Indicators		
	Base judgements on evidence and values	Evaluate judgements based on criteria	Defend solutions thoroughly

Handout A.12: Socratic Seminar Self-Reflection

Name: _____

Date: _____

| Something I did well is: | Something I wish I had done differently is: |

| This part of my thinking stayed the same: | This part of my thinking changed: |

How I feel Socratic Seminar went for our group today:

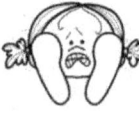   

Your opinion (feelings, questions, ideas, favorite parts) of this Socratic Seminar:

Handout A.13: Socratic Seminar Rubric

	Exemplary	**Proficient**	**Developing**	**Beginning**
Preparation	Student has read the text multiple times, taken notes, highlights key words or phrases.	Student has read the material and has a good understanding.	Student appears to have skimmed the article, but shows little reflection prior to the seminar.	Student is unprepared. Has not read the article or taken notes.
Content Knowledge	Student skillfully analyzes and interprets the information. Student provides meaningful references to the text.	Student compiles and interprets the information effectively. Student provides some references to the text.	Student compiles and lists facts from the text.. Student relies heavily on opinions but is unable to support with text.	Student requires teacher guidance to compile ideas. Requires frequent prompting.
Reasoning	Student cites relevant text evidence. Makes connections to other topics. Asks questions to further the dialogue. Willing to hear/take on other viewpoints.	Student cites some text evidence. Makes limited connections to others' ideas. May be able to hear other viewpoints.	Misses main points of the dialogue. May have some misunderstandings. Limited textual support. Refuses to acknowledge other viewpoints.	Comments do not make sense with the dialogue. Can't stay with the conversation..
Communicates thinking and reasoning effectively	Student is able to discuss thinking clearly, supporting claims with evidence and responding to claims of others. Builds on the ideas of others.	Student is able to discuss thinking clearly and support their own claims. May build on the ideas of others.	Student is able to discuss their own thinking clearly. Limited connecting or building upon the ideas of others.	Student participates in discussion, and is able to communicate effectively with teacher guidance.
Listening	Pays attention to details. Listens to others respectfully by making eye contact with the speaker and waiting their turn to speak. Asks for clarification.	Generally pays attention to others. Listens to others by making some eye contact with the speaker. May be too absorbed in their own ideas to actively engage in the discussion.	Appears to listen on and off throughout the seminar. May find some ideas unimportant and/or may be confused and not ask for clarification.	Student is uninvolved in the Socratic Seminar. Lots of misunderstanding due to inattention.
Conduct	Student demonstrates respect for others and follows the discussion. Participates but does not control the conversation.	Generally demonstrates respect for others and follows the discussion. May show some impatience with other view points. Avoids controlling the conversation.	Participates but tends to debate more than offer dialogue or is too timid to add to the conversation. May try to win. May engage in sidebar conversations.	Displays little respect for the learning process and interrupts frequently. Comments are not related or inappropriate.

Notes:

Appendix B
Extensions

Alternate Trade Books

In some cases, not all the trade books referenced within this unit may be readily available, or they may not be suited for your classroom environment, preferences, or audience. In other cases, you may choose to expand or deepen student understanding through an additional example rooted in rich text. Books listed in Table B.1 are suggestions for further study or to take the place of any of the read-aloud trade books suggested throughout the unit. Also included is a blackline master Read Aloud Reflection (Handout B.1), which can be used with any book of your choice to target the specified thinking skill.

TABLE B.1
Suggested Alternate Trade Books

Evaluative Thinking Sub-Skill	Suggested Alternate Trade Books/Guiding Questions

Considering Perspectives	❑ *They All Saw a Cat* by Brenden Wenzel
	  ■ How do we see things differently? The same?
	❑ *Guess Again!* by Mac Barnett
	  ■ How does our schema impact our perception/what we predict?
	❑ *Miss Nelson is Missing!* by Harry Allard
	  ■ How does perspective change with experience?
	❑ *Slow Loris* by Alexis Deacon
	  ■ What is missing from our perspective?

Developing Criteria	❑ *Frog and Toad are Friends* by Arnold Lobel
	  ■ What are the criteria for a good friend?
	❑ *Make Way for Ducklings* by Robert McCloskey
	  ■ What are the criteria for a duck's habitat? How does the book both succeed and fail at providing a suitable habitat for the ducks?
	❑ *Millions of Cats* by Wanda Gág
	  ■ What were the criteria for choosing a cat? Did the criteria vary based on the characters' perceptions?
	❑ *Alexander, Who Used to Be Rich Last Sunday* by Judith Viorst
	  ■ How could setting firm criteria and planning have helped Alexander?

Assigning Value	❑ *The Only Way is Badger* by Stella J. Jones
	  ■ What does it mean to be best? Are there things more valuable/important than being the best?
	❑ *Alexander, Who Used to be Rich Last Sunday* by Judith Viorst
	  ■ What is the value of money? How do you prioritize your spending?
	❑ *Things That Are Most in the World* by Judi Barrett
	  ■ An excellent study in superlatives!
	❑ *Extraordinary Jane* by Hannah E. Harrison
	  ■ What does it mean to be extraordinary? Is there more than one way to be great?
	❑ *The Day the Crayons Quit* by Drew Daywalt
	  ■ What is the value of each individual?

(Continued)

TABLE B.1
(Continued)

Evaluative Thinking Sub-Skill	Suggested Alternate Trade Books/Guiding Questions
Discussing Gray Area	❏ *Anansi and the Moss-Covered Rock* by Eric A. Kimmel ■ Is it ok to trick others for gain? What if you are tricking the trickster? ❏ *Thidwick the Big-Hearted Moose* by Dr. Seuss ■ Can we ever be too nice? ❏ *I am a Thief!* by Abigail Rayner ■ How harshly should we judge actions? Are there shades of right and wrong? ❏ *Hey, Little Ant* by Phillip M. Hoose ■ Is all life worth the same? Should we care for ants as much as people? ❏ *Jamaica's Find* by Juanita Havill ■ How can we listen to our conscience? ❏ *The Empty Pot* by Demi ■ How can we follow our values, even when they oppose our success? ❏ *Cheese Belongs to You!* by Alexis Deacon ■ What are the exceptions to rat law? ❏ *The Gruffalo* by Julia Donaldson ■ Is it ever ok to lie/mislead others?
Making and Defending Judgments	❏ *The Butter Battle Book* by Dr. Seuss ■ How can we defend judgments, even when it seems they are made for the wrong reasons? ❏ *The Trial of Cardigan Jones* by Tim Egan ■ How can we avoid rushing into a judgment? Are there consequences for jumping to conclusions? ❏ *You Choose* by Pippa Goodhart ■ This book gives options for making decisions on each page, and it comes in several variations, including space, dreams, and fairy tales, to give opportunities for choosing! ❏ *The Araboolies of Liberty Street* by Sam Swope ■ How can we make our own choices when we have pressure from society to conform? ❏ *Babu's Song* by Stephanie Stuve-Bodeen ■ How can we make choices that help others? ❏ *The Big Orange Splot* by Daniel Maus Pinkwater ■ How do our choices affect others?

Handout B.1: Universal Read Aloud Reflection
Book Title:

Name: _____

| Summarize the main idea of the story. | How did the book connect to the focus skill? |

What details from the text showcase the focus skill?

What patterns do you notice in your list from the question above?

What generalization (big idea) can you make about the focus skill based on this book?

Appendix B

Novel Study Extensions

Novels are a great way to extend learning about thinking skills, applying evaluative thinking in a broader context. The novels listed below support the thinking skills of this unit. The novel study units will allow the students to apply the thinking skills while reading excellent literature.

- *The One and Only Ivan* by Katherine Applegate
  - *The One and Only Ivan* tells the story of a gorilla who is held at a circus-themed mall. It raises many ethical and evaluative questions for students and gives unique perspectives to allow them to analyze gray area.
- *Amina's Voice* by Hena Khan
  - *Amina's Voice* is a story of a young Pakistani girl and how she uses her voice to build community. This novel provides many opportunities to judge perspectives and choices of others, as well as analyzing characters' motivations.
- *The Miraculous Journey of Edward Tulane* by Kate DiCamillo
  - This is a heartwarming story of a stuffed rabbit who is separated from his owner. Along his journey, he is under the care of many different people, who each impart a new identity to him. This novel examines the concepts of perspective, morality, and community, and how we come to gain and impart our values to others.
- *Stargirl* by Jerry Spinelli
  - *Stargirl* is the story of a school in Arizona where a new student drastically differs from the norm. It follows changing student reaction, and invites readers to think about ethical issues, values, and how important (or unimportant) it is to fit in with a crowd.
- *Fantastic Mr. Fox* by Roald Dahl
  - This story follows the plight of a fox family persecuted by angry farmers. It invites students to analyze the plans and solutions of both the foxes and the farmers, and to think through some gray ethical areas as well.

Games to Enhance Evaluative Thinking Skills

Many mass-market games can be used to hone evaluative thinking skills. Some suggested games which target evaluative thinking are listed here.

EVALUATIVE THINKING for Advanced Learners, Grades 3–5

- ❏ **Ticket to Ride** is a great strategy game that comes in several variations. In this game, players try to earn train routes by playing colored cards and finding their way across a map. This game supports evaluative thinking in that you must *develop criteria, assign value, consider perspectives*, and *make judgments* to play strategically.
- ❏ **Catan Jr.** is a strategy game in which players work to acquire resources and build their control of the island landscape. This game supports divergent thinking in that you must *develop criteria, discuss gray area*, and *make judgments* to strategically move and build around the board.
- ❏ **Chess** is a classic strategy game that appeals to all ages. This game supports evaluative thinking in that you must *consider perspectives, assign value*, and *make judgments* in developing a strategy of movement for various chess pieces throughout the game.
- ❏ **Qwirkle** is a game that combines visual-spatial skills with evaluative thinking. In this game, players place tiles in a grid pattern based upon their attributes. The longer a connection of similar tiles, the more points a player can score. The game supports evaluative thinking in that you must *consider various perspectives, develop criteria, assign value*, and *make judgments* as to how to place tiles most strategically while preventing your opponents from doing the same.
- ❏ **Azul** is a strategy game in which players compete for high scores by placing decorative tiles on the board and claiming spaces. Players can earn points for patterning or making sets but may also incur penalties for illegal moves. This game supports divergent thinking in that you must use forward thinking to *consider various perspectives, develop criteria, assign value*, and *make judgments* as to how to place tiles most strategically while preventing your opponents from doing the same.

For Product Safety Concerns and Information please contact our EU representative GPSR@taylorandfrancis.com
Taylor & Francis Verlag GmbH, Kaufingerstraße 24, 80331 München, Germany

www.ingramcontent.com/pod-product-compliance
Lightning Source LLC
Chambersburg PA
CBHW080937300426
44115CB00017B/2853